Cookie

cook·ie [kook-ee], noun

······································

100 essential recipes

spruce

An Hachette UK Company
www.hachette.co.uk

First published in Great Britain in 2014 by Spruce
A division of Octopus Publishing Group Ltd
Endeavour House, 189 Shaftesbury Avenue, London, WC2H 8JY
www.octopusbooks.co.uk
www.octopusbooksusa.com

Distributed in the US by Hachette Book Group USA
237 Park Avenue, New York NY 10017 USA

Distributed in Canada by Canadian Manda Group
165 Dufferin Street, Toronto, Ontario, Canada M6K 3H6

ISBN 978 1 84601 430 7

Printed and bound in China

10 9 8 7 6 5 4 3 2 1

CONSULTANT PUBLISHER Sarah Ford
EDITOR Jo Wilson
COPY EDITOR Jo Richardson
DESIGNER Eoghan O'Brien & Clare Barber
ILLUSTRATOR Abigail Read
PRODUCTION CONTROLLER Sarah Connelly

CONTENTS

Introduction **6**

Everyday Cookies **12**

Fruity & Nutty **44**

Chocolate Cookies **70**

Decorated Cookies **100**

Savory Cookies **122**

With a Twist **138**

Index **156**

Glossary & Picture Credits **160**

INTRODUCTION

There is nothing more satisfying than baking a batch of homemade cookies. From choosing the recipe and mixing the ingredients to shaping the dough and picking out decorations, the whole process is a joy. Then, of course, there is the sense of anticipation as the glorious aroma seeps around the house and finally it is time to sample the freshly baked cookies, still warm from the oven.

Cookies are extremely versatile, as the recipes in this book demonstrate. You can prepare a quick batch of chocolate cookies for an after-school treat, or you can rustle up more intricately decorated cookies for gifts and special occasions. Many of the recipes are quick and easy to prepare, which means the whole family can get involved. Kids love mixing and decorating—and, of course, sampling their creations—and homemade cookies are a great introduction to baking. Whether you are a novice baker or an experienced cook, you will discover recipes for every occasion that everyone will enjoy.

ESSENTIAL EQUIPMENT

One of the great things about baking cookies is that you don't need to go out and spend a fortune on special equipment. You will probably already own most of the baking equipment you need to get started on many of the recipes in this book. If you plan to create some of the more highly decorated cookies, you will also need a selection of pastry bags and other decorating tools, but for the majority of recipes the following essential equipment will be sufficient.

MIXING BOWLS

It's a good idea to have a selection of sizes, because many recipes require more than one mixing bowl.

MEASURING

Baking generally requires precise measurements, which makes a good set of kitchen measuring cups indispensable. They come in ¼, ⅓, ½, and 1 cup sizes—and you should also have a set of measuring spoons, from ¼ teaspoon to 1 tablespoon. When measuring a dry ingredient, use the back edge of a blunt knife to level it, and for brown sugar, pack it in firmly before leveling it. A large see-through measuring cup is useful for liquids. When measuring, keep it on a flat surface and view the measurement lines on the side of the cup at eye level for accuracy.

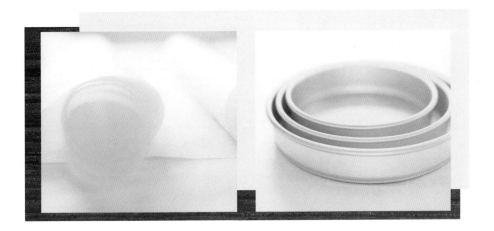

COOKIE SHEETS

It is a good idea to have a number of good-quality cookie sheets to hand. Cookie dough expands a lot during cooking, so always space the cookies widely. This often means using more than one cookie sheet for a batch of cookies.

PARCHMENT PAPER

Some recipes call for a greased cookie sheet and others require you to line the cookie sheet with parchment paper.

COOKIE CUTTERS

These are essential for any cookie enthusiast. Some of the recipes call for specific cutter sizes or shapes, but you can also choose your own—festive, animal, and character shapes can be used for everyday baking, and letter cutters are ideal for gift cookies.

WIRE RACK

Although some batches of cookies will barely make it out of the oven before being eaten, there will be times when you need a wire rack for cooling down.

KEY INGREDIENTS

With this short list of ingredients you can create basic cookie dough.

- **All-purpose flour**
- **Eggs**—the fresher the better
- **Baking powder** and/or baking soda
- **Fat**—this could be butter, margarine, or oil
- **Sugar**—keep a stock of superfine, granulated, and brown sugars

To make your own superfine sugar, put the same quantity of granulated sugar in a food processor and blend for a minute. If you add a few more pantry staples (such as unsweetened cocoa powder, powdered sugar, vanilla extract, citrus fruit, dried fruits, and nuts), your repertoire will expand greatly and you will be able to choose from a variety of recipes in the book without heading out to the grocery store.

Obviously, if you have a particular recipe in mind, you will need to make a shopping list and get yourself prepped in advance.

BASIC TECHNIQUES

Cookie recipes use many of the same baking techniques to ensure the ingredients are well combined, the dough is workable, and the baked product is successful. It is, therefore, a good idea to familiarize yourself with these basics before you start cooking.

BEATING EGG WHITES

There's a skill to achieving perfectly light and fluffy egg whites.

- Make sure the mixing bowl is spotlessly clean and don't use a plastic bowl
- Always use fresh eggs and let them come to room temperature
- Start whisking slowly, then build up speed as the eggs start to thicken
- Be patient—it takes time to achieve soft peaks
- As soon as the eggs are fluffy, stop beating or they will begin to turn liquid again
- Use the beaten egg whites immediately upon beating them

CREAMING

Creaming is the process of combining the fat and sugar in a recipe. You can cream ingredients in a food mixer, but many people prefer to control the process by doing it by hand.

- Begin with the butter or margarine at room temperature
- Start mixing slowly, then increase the speed as the ingredients begin to combine
- The dough should become soft, light, and pale. The volume will increase as the ingredients fully combine

GREASING A COOKIE SHEET

- You can use a small piece of parchment paper or a pastry brush to grease the cookie sheet(s)
- Work methodically over the sheet, and up and around the edges, to make sure that the whole area is covered in a thin, even layer of fat
- If you lift the sheet to the light, you will be able to see any overlooked areas

LINING A COOKIE SHEET

Cookie dough is delicate and lining the cookie sheet will help the cookies slide off in one piece.

- You can use parchment paper or reusable silicone pan liners
- Cut the paper to fit exactly on the bottom of the cookie sheet, going right up to the edges
- If you draw around the bottom of the sheet, you will get an exact fit and avoid retrimming

ROLLING OUT DOUGH

- Before you start rolling, liberally spread flour onto the work surface and all over the rolling pin
- Cookie dough can be sticky— use a ceramic rolling pin instead of a wooden one
- You will achieve a more even thickness if you roll out from the middle of the dough
- Sprinkle more flour over the dough and rolling pin as you roll to stop it from sticking

SHAPING COOKIE DOUGH

Different recipes call for different approaches to shaping the cookies. Some recipes require scoops of dough to be placed on the cookie sheets; for others, you will need to shape the dough by hand.

- You can use a scoop to measure out even amounts of dough
- Gently roll the dough in your hands to form even balls—if there is too much or too little dough, just add or remove some and reroll
- Aim for even shapes, otherwise the cookies won't bake evenly

PIPING COOKIE DOUGH

This is another technique used in a number of cookie recipes and it helps to ensure that the cookies are even sizes and evenly spaced.

- Use two hands—one to squeeze the pastry bag and one to direct the dough
- Keep the dough pushed down toward the decorating tip so there are no gaps
- Stop piping before you move the bag away from the cookie

STORING AND FREEZING

It takes a little practice to create perfect batches of cookies every time, but if you follow the recipes carefully, you will master the art in no time at all.

Of course, a fresh sheet of cookies will probably disappear as soon as it is taken out of the oven, which means storage won't be an issue. However, if you do manage to hold some back, here are some tips on storage.

STORING

If you are making large batches of cookies, it is important to store them correctly so they stay fresh. Keep a stock of airtight containers ready to transfer your cookies once they have cooled and try to separate the cookies, depending on their texture and consistency; softer cookies can be carefully stacked in airtight containers, whereas glazed or decorated cookies should be stored in upright layers, in between sheets of parchment paper.

FREEZING

Most cookies freeze well, and it is a good idea to cook them in large batches, then tuck some out of sight for when the family has a cookie craving or to offer unexpected visitors. Transfer the cooled cookies to airlock freezer bags or airtight containers, label with the date and type, and they will stay fresh in the freezer for up to three months.

You can also freeze cookie dough, which means you can enjoy freshly baked cookies at a moment's notice. Once the dough is prepared, roll it into cookie balls and place these spaced apart on a cookie sheet, making sure they are all the same size. Now place the cookie sheets in the freezer until the cookie dough balls have frozen—this stops them from sticking together. Transfer the cookie dough balls to freezer bags or airtight containers and keep in the freezer for up to three months. When it's time to bake them, let them defrost, then bake as normal.

DECORATING

You don't need an art diploma to create eye-catching designs—simple icing tops or chocolate dips will make your cookies stand out. You can be as intricate and as imaginative as you want with characters, festive designs, faces, and piping.

ROYAL ICING

The consistency of the icing will depend on the design you want to create. If you are covering the whole cookie (flooding), the icing should be fairly loose; for detailed work, you should use a firmer paste. Prepare the icing in advance, especially if you are using two or more colors. Let the cookies cool down on lined cookie sheets before icing. Put ⅓ cup royal icing sugar and 6 tablespoons of water in a bowl and beat together to make a thick paste to spread on cookies. Leave in a cool place to set for 30 minutes.

QUICK BUTTERCREAM

For a foolpoof icing, buttercream wins hands-down. Beat together 1 cup confectioner's sugar with 6 tablespoons unsalted butter and 1 teaspoon of hot water until creamy.

PASTRY BAGS

You will need a selection of these and a variety of decorating tips that will suit different cookie sizes and decoration styles. As a general rule, no. 2 tips should be used for average-size cookies—move up or down a size for bigger or smaller cookies.

TEMPLATES

There are as many templates available as there are decorating ideas, and these are a great way to get the basic shape and design of your decoration onto the cookie. Templates come in all shapes, sizes, and materials. You can make your own, and some are reusable plastic or metal molds that make an imprint on the top of the cookie; others are paper ones that are cut out.

GIFTS

Cookies make great gifts because they can be personalized for virtually any occasion. Use number templates for birthday cookies, or create a design that relates to the profession or hobby of the recipient—football, ballet shoes, cars, book covers ... the list is endless.

When it comes to packaging the cookies, there are a lot of quirky ideas to show them off. Here are a few:

- Canning jars
- Cellophane bags tied with bright ribbon
- Gift boxes lined with tissue paper
- Bakery boxes
- Paper cones
- Decorated envelopes
- Inside a cup or glass wrapped in cellophane (two gifts in one)

TOP TEN TIPS

1. Read the recipe
• It might sound obvious, but it's important to read all the way through the recipe before you begin—one missing ingredient or piece of equipment could mean a batch of substandard cookies.

2. Preheat the oven
• Your oven needs to be at the correct temperature as soon as your cookies are ready to bake, so turn it on before you begin.

3. Measure with care
• Baking is an exact science and all ingredients need to be carefully measured for the perfect results.

4. Soften butter
• Take the butter out of refrigerator about an hour before cooking so that it is at room temperature when you reach the creaming part of the recipe.

5. Chill the dough
• Chill the dough in the refrigerator for about an hour (or 15–20 minutes in the freezer) to dry it out. You should also keep your hands cool— if the dough warms up, it melts and will be difficult to work with.

6. Flour power
• Cookie dough is sticky and a warm kitchen and warm hands make it even stickier. Use plenty of flour on the work surface and rolling pin to keep the dough in check.

7. Equal sizes
• Make sure each piece of cookie dough is the same size—if not, you will end up with some overcooked and some undercooked cookies in your batch.

8. Room to expand
• Always leave plenty of space between the cookies on the cookie sheet, otherwise the dough will merge as it expands. Use extra sheets if you're not sure.

9. Baking times
• Always double-check baking times and check the cookies a couple of minutes before the end, because ovens do vary. An undercooked cookie can be put back in the oven, but there's no rescue for an overcooked one.

10. Cooling down
• Let the cookies completely cool before storing them.

THUMBPRINT COOKIES P30

EVERYDAY
COOKIES

SUNFLOWER SEED COOKIES

- -

MAKES 30

- ½ cup (1 stick) salted butter, plus extra for greasing
- ½ cup firmly packed light brown sugar
- 2 tablespoons honey
- 1 cup all-purpose flour
- 1 teaspoon baking powder
- 1⅓ cups rolled oats
- ½ teaspoon baking soda
- ½ cup sunflower seed
- ½ teaspoon ground ginger

1. Preheat the oven to 350°F and lightly grease two cookie sheets.

2. Cut the butter into large pieces and put in a saucepan with the sugar and honey. Heat gently until the butter has melted.

3. Remove from the heat and stir in the flour, baking powder, oats, baking soda, sunflower seed, and ginger, beating well to mix.

4. Take heaping teaspoonfuls of the dough and shape coarsely into balls. Space the balls well apart on the prepared cookie sheets and flatten slightly. Bake in the preheated oven for 12–15 minutes or until risen and lightly brown. Let sit on the cookie sheets for a few minutes to slightly harden, then transfer to a wire rack to cool completely.

MELTING MOMENTS

- - - - - - - - - - - - - - - - - - - -

Summery, zingy, and very delicious, these refreshing cookies are perfect with Earl Grey tea or cordial at a summer picnic.

MAKES 20
- ¾ cup (1½ sticks) butter, softened, plus extra for greasing
- ¼ cup granulated sugar
- 1 egg yolk
- 1⅓ cups all-purpose flour
- Grated zest of ½ orange or lemon
- 1 tablespoon orange or lemon juice
- Candied peel, for decoration
- Confectioners' sugar, for dusting

1. Preheat the oven to 375°F and lightly grease two cookie sheets.

2. Cream together the butter and sugar until light and fluffy. Beat in the egg yolk. Work in the flour and orange or lemon zest and juice to form a smooth, thick paste.

3. Spoon the paste into a pastry bag fitted with a large star tip and pipe rosettes measuring about 2 inches across onto the prepared cookie sheets. Lightly press some candied peel into each cookie.

4. Bake in the preheated oven for 15–20 minutes, until lightly brown. Let sit on the cookie sheets for a few minutes to slightly harden, then transfer to a wire rack to cool completely. Dust each cookie with confectioners' sugar.

LANGUES DE CHAT

MAKES 20-24
- 4 tablespoons butter, plus extra for greasing
- ¼ cup superfine sugar
- 2 egg whites
- ⅓ cup plus 1 tablespoon all-purpose flour, sifted, plus extra for dusting
- A few drops of vanilla extract

1. Preheat the oven to 400°F and lightly grease and flour a cookie sheet.

2. Cream together the butter and sugar until light and fluffy. Whisk the egg whites lightly and gradually beat into the creamed mixture. Carefully fold in the flour and vanilla extract.

3. Place the batter in a pastry bag fitted with a ¾-inch plain tip and pipe 3-inch lengths on the prepared cookie sheet.

4. Bake in the preheated oven for 10 minutes, until the cookies are pale golden but darker around the edges. Let sit on the cookie sheet for a few minutes to slightly harden, then transfer to a wire rack to cool completely.

CINNAMON GINGER COOKIES

MAKES 12

- ¾ cup plus 1 tablespoon all-purpose flour
- 1 teaspoon baking powder
- ½ teaspoon baking soda
- ½ teaspoon ground cinnamon
- ½ teaspoon ground ginger
- ¼ teaspoon ground allspice or apple pie spice
- Finely grated zest of 1 lemon
- 4 tablespoons butter, diced, plus extra for greasing
- ¼ cup superfine sugar
- 2 tablespoons light corn syrup

1. Preheat the oven to 350°F and lightly grease two large cookie sheets.

2. Mix together the flour, baking powder, baking soda, spices, and lemon zest in a mixing bowl. Add the butter and rub in with your fingertips until the mixture resembles fine bread crumbs.

3. Stir in the sugar and add the syrup. Mix together, first with a spoon, then squeeze the crumbs together with your hands to form a ball. Shape the dough into a log, then slice into 12. Roll each piece into a ball and arrange on the prepared cookie sheets, leaving space between for them to spread during cooking.

4. Cook one cookie sheet at a time in the center of the preheated oven for 8–10 minutes or until the cookie tops are cracked and golden. Let sit on the cookie sheet for a few minutes to slightly harden, then transfer to a wire rack to cool completely.

> **TIP**
>
> • For chocolate ginger yo-yos, use 1 teaspoon ground ginger instead of the three spices and the grated zest of ½ small orange instead of 1 lemon. Shape into 20 small cookies, bake for 5–6 minutes as above, then transfer to a wire rack to cool. Melt 3 oz semisweet chocolate, then sandwich cookies together. Drizzle the rest over the top of the cookies. Serve when the chocolate has hardened.

CLASSIC SHORTBREAD

MAKES 16

- ¾ cup plus 2 tablespoons (1¾ sticks) unsalted butter, at room temperature
- ⅔ cup superfine sugar, plus extra for sprinkling
- 2 cups all-purpose flour, plus extra for dusting
- ¾ cup rice flour
- Pinch of salt

1. Preheat the oven to 375°F.

2. Beat together the butter and sugar in a mixing bowl or a food processor until pale and creamy. Sift in the flour, rice flour, and salt and mix or process briefly until the ingredients just come together.

3. Transfer to a work surface and knead lightly to form a soft dough. Shape into a circle, wrap in plastic wrap, and chill for 30 minutes.

4. Divide the dough in half and roll out each piece on a lightly floured surface to an 8-inch circle. Transfer to two ungreased cookie sheets. Score each circle with a sharp knife, marking it into 8 equal wedges, prick with a fork, and use your fingers to flute the edges.

5. Sprinkle with a little superfine sugar and bake in the preheated oven for 18–20 minutes, until golden. Remove from the oven and, while still hot, cut into wedges through the score marks. Let sit on the cookie sheets for 5 minutes, then transfer to a wire rack to cool completely.

TANGY APPLE SQUARES

MAKES 18

- Butter, for greasing
- 1 large Granny Smith or other cooking apple
- 2 egg yolks
- 3 tablespoons lemon juice
- 2 teaspoons cornstarch
- ¼ teaspoon ground cinnamon
- ⅓ cup superfine sugar, plus extra for sprinkling
- 1 lb puff pastry
- All-purpose flour, for dusting
- ½ cup confectioners' sugar

1. Preheat the oven to 400°F and lightly grease a large cookie sheet.

2. Peel, core, and grate the apple into a small saucepan. Beat in one of the egg yolks, 2 tablespoons of the lemon juice, the cornstarch, cinnamon, and sugar. Heat gently, stirring, until the juices have thickened. Turn into a bowl and let cool.

3. Thinly roll out the pastry on a lightly floured surface to a 14-inch square and cut in half. Beat the remaining egg yolk with 1 teaspoon of water and brush a little over one half of the pastry. Place on the prepared cookie sheet.

4. Spoon the apple mixture over the pastry, spreading it almost to the edges. Position the second rectangle of pastry on top. Cut the pastry lengthwise into three strips, then across into squares, but don't separate the squares. Brush the top with the egg yolk. Bake in the preheated oven for 25 minutes, until puffed and golden. Let cool on the cookie sheet. Separate the pieces with a knife.

5. Put the confectioners' sugar in a bowl and beat in enough of the remaining lemon juice until the icing thinly coats the back of the spoon. Drizzle the icing back and forth over the squares.

JAPONAIS

MAKES 8

- ½ cup ground almonds
- ⅔ cup superfine sugar
- 2 egg whites

Coffee filling

- 3 tablespoons butter
- ⅔ cup confectioners' sugar, sifted
- 1 teaspoon milk
- 1 teaspoon coffee extract

To decorate

- ¼ cup ground almonds, browned
- Confectioners' sugar

1. Preheat the oven to 300°F and line a cookie sheet with parchment paper.

2. Mix together the almonds and sugar and set aside. Whisk the egg whites until stiff, then fold in the almond mixture.

3. Spoon the batter into a pastry bag fitted with a ½-inch plain tip and pipe sixteen 2-inch circles on the prepared cookie sheet. Bake in the preheated oven for 30–35 minutes. Let sit for a few minutes to slightly harden, then transfer to a wire rack and let cool completely.

4. To make the coffee filling, cream the butter with half of the confectioners' sugar until soft, then add the milk, coffee extract, and the remaining confectioners' sugar. Beat well.

5. Sandwich the circles together in pairs with some of the coffee filling and spread more around the sides. Press ground almonds around the side of each cookie. Let set, then dust with confectioners' sugar.

LEMON COOKIES

MAKES 25-30

- I cup (2 sticks) unsalted butter, softened, plus extra for greasing
- ½ cup superfine sugar
- Grated zest of 2 lemons
- I tablespoon lemon juice
- 2⅓ cups plus I tablespoon all-purpose flour
- 2½ teaspoons baking powder

1. Preheat the oven to 350°F and lightly grease three large cookie sheets.

2. Put the butter, sugar, lemon zest, and juice in a bowl and, using an electric hand mixer, beat together until pale and light. Sift in the flour and baking powder and continue beating to form a stiff dough.

3. Roll 25-30 pieces of dough into balls and flatten them into 2-inch circles. Score the surface of each one with the back of fork and put them on the prepared cookie sheets. Bake in the preheated oven for 12–15 minutes, until lightly golden. Let sit on the cookie sheets for a few minutes to slightly harden, then transfer to a wire rack to cool completely.

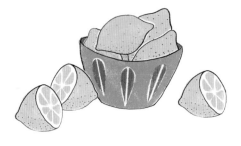

JELLY-FILLED COOKIES

- - - - - - - - - - - - - - - - - - -

These jelly-filled cookies are best eaten on the day they are baked. You can use preserves instead of jelly, and choose other flavors, such as strawberry or grape.

MAKES ABOUT 48
- ¾ cup (1½ sticks) unsalted butter, softened, plus extra for greasing
- 1¼ cups superfine sugar
- 1 egg, lightly beaten
- 1 teaspoon almond extract
- 2 cups all-purpose flour
- ½ teaspoon baking powder
- 1¼ cups ground almonds
- ⅓ cup raspberry jelly

1. Preheat the oven to 350°F and lightly grease two large cookie sheets.

2. Put the butter and sugar in a bowl and, using an electric hand mixer, beat together until light and fluffy. Beat in the egg and almond extract until combined. Sift in the flour and baking powder and use a wooden spoon to stir into the creamed mixture with the ground almonds to form a soft dough.

3. Break off small walnut-size pieces of dough, shape them into balls, and flatten them slightly to 1½-inch circles. Transfer them to the prepared cookie sheets, spacing them well apart, and make an indentation in the center of each one with your thumb.

4. Spoon ¼ teaspoon of jelly into the hollow centers and bake in the preheated oven for 10–12 minutes or until lightly golden. Let sit on the cookie sheets for a few minutes to slightly harden, then transfer to a wire rack to cool completely. Repeat with the remaining dough to make about 48 cookies.

MOTHER'S OAT BARS

These wholesome treats are great for an afternoon snack to bridge the gap between lunch and dinner. They will keep in an airtight container for up to a week.

MAKES 16
- ½ cup (1 stick) unsalted butter, softened plus extra for greasing
- ½ cup vegetable shortening
- ½ cup demerara or other raw sugar
- ¼ cup light corn syrup
- 4 cups rolled oats

1. Preheat the oven to 325°F. Grease and line the bottom of a 9 x 13-inch jellyroll pan.

2. Put the butter, shortening, sugar, and corn syrup into a saucepan and heat gently, stirring, until the butter and shortening are melted and the sugar has dissolved. Remove from the heat and stir in the oats until evenly coated.

3. Transfer the dough to the prepared pan and spread it flat. Bake in the preheated oven for 35 minutes, until a deep golden all over. Remove from the oven and immediately score into 16 bars. Let cool in the pan, then cut into bars.

PRESERVED GINGER PUMPKIN COOKIES

- - - - - - - - - - - - - - - - - - - -

MAKES ABOUT 24
- 8-oz piece seeded pumpkin
- ½ cup (1 stick) salted butter, softened, plus extra for greasing
- ¾ cup demerara or other raw sugar, plus extra for sprinkling
- 1 egg
- 1¼ cups rolled oats
- ¾ cup all-purpose flour
- 1 teaspoon baking powder
- 3 pieces preserved ginger in syrup, drained and finely chopped
- ⅓ cup pumpkin seeds

1. Preheat the oven to 375°F and lightly grease two cookie sheets.

2. Cut away the skin from the pumpkin and finely grate the flesh. Pat dry between plenty of layers of paper towel until the pumpkin feels dry.

3. Beat together the butter and sugar until smooth and creamy. Beat in the pumpkin, then the egg, oats, flour, baking powder, chopped ginger, and 3 tablespoons of the pumpkin seeds until the ingredients are evenly combined.

4. Place heaping teaspoonfuls of the dough on the prepared cookie sheets, spacing them well apart. Sprinkle with the remaining seeds.

5. Bake in the preheated oven for 15 minutes or until golden around the edges. Sprinkle with extra sugar and let sit on the cookie sheets for a few minutes to slightly harden. Transfer to a wire rack to cool completely.

STICKY GINGER COOKIES

- -

These sticky, chewy cookies are the perfect nostalgic treat—great with a cup of a hot chocolate during the winter months.

MAKES 18
- 1 large egg
- ⅓ cup firmly packed light brown sugar
- 2 tablespoons black molasses
- 4 tablespoons salted butter, melted
- 2 tablespoons milk
- 1¼ cups all-purpose flour
- ¼ teaspoon baking soda
- 2 teaspoons ground ginger
- ¼ cup ginger marmalade or preserves
- Confectioners' sugar, for dusting

1. Line a large cookie sheet with parchment paper. Put the egg, sugar, and molasses in a bowl and beat well until thickened and foamy. Beat in the butter and milk.

2. Sift the flour, baking soda, and ginger into the bowl and stir well to mix. Spoon heaping teaspoonfuls of the mixture onto the prepared cookie sheet, spacing them well apart.

3. Bake in a preheated oven, at 375°F, for 15 minutes or until well risen but still soft. Let cool on the baking sheets for 5 minutes, until a little firm, then transfer to a wire rack to cool.

4. Press the ginger marmalade or preserves through a strainer into a small saucepan and heat gently to make a smooth glaze. Brush over the cooled cookies and dust with confectioners' sugar.

CHERRY & ALMOND COOKIES

MAKES 18
- 2½ cups all-purpose flour, plus extra for dusting
- 1 cup plus 2 tablespoons (2¼ sticks) salted butter, cut into pieces
- ⅔ cup granulated sugar
- 1 teaspoon cold water
- ¼ cup strawberry or cherry preserves
- 1 cup ground almonds
- 2 large eggs
- 1¾ teaspoons baking powder
- 1 teaspoon almond extract
- ¾ cup halved natural candied cherries
- ¼ cup slivered almonds
- Confectioners' sugar, for dusting

1. Line a 12½ x 7 inch shallow baking pan (or similar size roasting pan) with a rectangle of parchment paper, fitting the paper into the corners. Put half the flour in a food processor and add ½ cup (1 stick) of the butter, cut into pieces. Blend until the mixture resembles bread crumbs. Add ¼ cup of the sugar and the measured cold water and blend to a paste.

2. Roll out the paste on a lightly floured surface until roughly the same size as the pan bottom. Lift into the prepared pan and flatten out in an even layer. Bake in a preheated oven, at 350°F, for 25 minutes, until pale golden.

3. Spread the pastry with the preserves in an even layer. Beat together the remaining butter and sugar with the ground almonds, eggs, remaining flour, baking powder, and almond extract until smooth and creamy. Stir in the candied cherries and spread over the pastry bottom.

4. Sprinkle with the slivered almonds and bake for 25 minutes until just firm to the touch and golden. Leave to cool in the pan. Dust with confectioners' sugar and serve cut into squares.

THUMBPRINT COOKIES

These cookies are light and incredibly crumbly with a rich slick of chocolate filling in the centers.

MAKES 14-16

- ½ cup (1 stick) unsalted butter, slightly softened
- ⅓ cup superfine sugar
- 1 egg, beaten
- 1 cup all-purpose flour
- ½ teaspoon baking powder
- ½ cup ground almonds
- 1 tablespoon unsweetened cocoa powder, sifted

- 1 tablespoon cornstarch
- Pinch of salt

Chocolate icing
- 3 oz semisweet chocolate (50 percent cocoa), broken into pieces
- 2 tablespoons vegetable oil

1. Cream together the butter and sugar until light and fluffy. Beat in the egg.

2. Mix the remaining cookie ingredients and gently work into the butter mixture. Chill for 1 hour until firm—it makes it easier to roll into balls. Preheat the oven to 350°F.

3. Take tablespoons of the dough and form into balls. Press firmly with a thumb to make deep indentations in the centers. Place on a nonstick cookie sheet and bake in the preheated oven for 10–12 minutes, until firm. Place on a wire rack to cool completely.

4. When the cookies have cooled, melt the chocolate in a heatproof bowl over a saucepan of simmering water, or microwave for 1–2 minutes. Let cool a little, then stir in the oil. Pour a teaspoon of chocolate into the center of each cookie and let harden.

MAPLE SYRUP OAT BARS

Not only is maple syrup the most natural form of sweetener there is, it also avoids the sugar highs and lows of other sweeteners. These bars make a perfect mid-morning snack.

MAKES 12
- ¾ cup sunflower margarine, plus 2 tablespoons, plus extra for greasing
- ½ cup maple syrup
- ⅔ cup firmly packed light brown sugar
- 3⅔ cups rolled oats

1. Preheat the oven to 350°F. Grease a 6½ x 10 x 1½-inch baking pan and line it with parchment paper, snipping it diagonally in the corners so it fits snugly over the bottom and up the sides.

2. Put the margarine in a medium saucepan over medium heat and melt. Stir in the maple syrup and sugar, and let simmer until the sugar is mostly dissolved. Remove from the heat and stir in the oats.

3. Spoon the batter into the prepared pan and bake in the preheated oven for 25 minutes. Let sit in the pan for a few minutes to slightly harden, then cut into bars while still warm. Let cool completely, then remove from the parchment paper and lift out with a metal spatula.

CUSTARD
CREAMS

MAKES 14
- 1 cup all-purpose flour, plus extra for dusting
- ¼ cup custard powder
- ¾ cup (1½ sticks) salted butter, cut into pieces,
  plus extra for greasing
- ¾ cup confectioners' sugar
- 1 egg yolk

1. Put the flour and 3 tablespoons of the custard powder in a food processor and add ½ cup (1 stick) of the butter, cut into pieces. Blend until the mixture resembles bread crumbs. Add ½ cup of the sugar and the egg yolk and blend to a paste. Wrap and chill for at least 1 hour.

2. Meanwhile, preheat the oven to 350°F and lightly grease a large cookie sheet. Thinly roll out the dough on a lightly floured surface until large enough to cut out a 10½-inch square. Lift onto the prepared cookie sheet and trim off the uneven edges to shape a neat square. Mark the rectangle lengthwise into 1½-inch strips, then make three evenly spaced cuts in the opposite direction so you end up with 28 rectangles. Prick all over with a fork.

3. Bake in the preheated oven for 15 minutes, until pale golden around the edges. Let sit in the pan for 5 minutes, then re-mark the cuts with a knife and separate the cookies. If the cookies are very pale in the center, return them to the oven for another few minutes. Transfer to a wire rack to cool.

4. Soften the remaining butter and beat with the remaining sugar and custard powder until smooth and creamy, adding ½ teaspoon hot water if the icing is too firm. Use to sandwich the rectangles together.

WAFER
SNAPS

MAKES 18-20

- 3 egg whites
- ⅓ cup superfine sugar
- 2 tablespoons unsalted butter, melted, plus extra for greasing
- ⅓ cup all-purpose flour
- 2 tablespoons light cream

1. Preheat the oven to 375°F. Line two cookie sheets with parchment paper and lightly grease the paper.

2. Beat together the egg whites and sugar until the egg whites are broken up. Stir in the melted butter, flour, and cream to form a smooth batter.

3. Spoon 6 scant tablespoonfuls of the batter, spaced well apart, onto the prepared cookie sheet and spread each with the back of the spoon to a circle about 2½ inches in diameter.

4. Bake in the preheated oven for 7–8 minutes or until the edges are turning golden brown. Peel the cookies off the paper and place over a rolling pin to set before transferring to a wire rack.

5. Make more cookies using the remaining batter. (If they've started to harden on the cookie sheet before you've had a chance to shape them, put them back in the oven briefly to soften.)

BISCOTTI

These twice-baked Italian cookies are ideal to serve at the end of a dinner party—try dipping them into coffee or dessert wine for a delicious end to the meal.

MAKES ABOUT 28

- 4 tablespoons salted butter, softened, plus extra for greasing
- ¼ cup superfine sugar
- 1½ cups all-purpose flour, plus extra for dusting
- 2½ teaspoons baking powder
- ½ teaspoon ground coriander
- Finely grated zest of 1 orange, plus 1 tablespoon juice
- ⅓ cup cornmeal
- 1 egg, lightly beaten
- ⅔ cup unblanched almonds, coarsely chopped

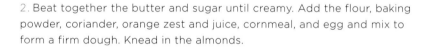

1. Preheat the oven to 325°F and lightly grease a large cookie sheet.

2. Beat together the butter and sugar until creamy. Add the flour, baking powder, coriander, orange zest and juice, cornmeal, and egg and mix to form a firm dough. Knead in the almonds.

3. Turn out the dough onto a lightly floured surface and knead lightly until evenly mixed. Divide the dough in half and shape each piece into a log about 9 inches long. Place on the prepared cookie sheet, spacing them well apart, and flatten each to a depth of about ¾ inch.

4. Bake in the preheated oven for 30–35 minutes or until risen and just firm. Let cool on the cookie sheet for 15 minutes, then transfer to a board and, using a serrated knife, cut across into ½-inch-thick slices.

5. Arrange on the cookie sheet, cut sides down, and bake for an additional 10–15 minutes, until crisp. Using a spatula, transfer to a wire rack to cool.

PIPED COOKIES

MAKES ABOUT 12
- ¾ cup (1½ sticks) unsalted butter, softened, plus extra for greasing
- ¼ cup superfine sugar
- 1 teaspoon vanilla extract
- 2 cups all-purpose flour
- 1 tablespoon milk

1. Preheat the oven to 350°F and lightly grease two cookie sheets.

2. Beat together the butter, sugar, and vanilla extract until pale and creamy. Add the flour and milk and mix to form a smooth batter.

3. Put the batter in a large pastry bag fitted with a large star or plain tip. Pipe fingers, rings, or squiggles of dough, spaced slightly apart, onto the prepared cookie sheets.

4. Bake in the preheated oven for 15–20 minutes or until slightly risen and just beginning to darken. Let sit on the cookie sheets for a few minutes to slightly harden, then transfer to a wire rack to cool completely.

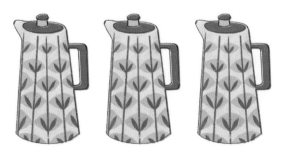

CHUNKY OAT COOKIES

MAKES ABOUT 12

- ½ cup (I stick) unsalted butter, plus extra for greasing
- ½ cup superfine sugar
- I tablespoon light corn syrup
- I cup rolled oats
- I cup all-purpose flour
- I teaspoon baking powder
- ½ teaspoon baking soda

1. Preheat the oven to 350°F and lightly grease a large cookie sheet.

2. Put the butter, sugar, and corn syrup into a saucepan and heat gently until the butter has melted. Remove from the heat and stir in the oats, flour, baking powder, and baking soda until well mixed. Transfer to a bowl and let sit for a few minutes until cool enough to handle.

3. Shape heaping teaspoonfuls of the dough into balls and place on the prepared cookie sheet, spacing them well apart. Flatten each slightly with the back of a fork and bake in the preheated oven for 15–20 minutes, until the cookies have spread slightly and are pale golden. Let sit on the cookie sheet for a few minutes to slightly harden, then transfer to a wire rack to cool completely.

CARDAMOM & ORANGE MADELEINES

- - - - - - - - - - - - - - -

The exotic citrus and spice flavors of these delicate bakes are sure to impress your friends.

MAKES ABOUT 24 COOKIES

- 2 teaspoons cardamom pods
- 3 eggs
- ½ cup superfine sugar
- Finely grated zest of 1 small orange, plus 1–2 tablespoons juice
- 1 cup all-purpose flour, plus extra for dusting
- 1½ teaspoons baking powder
- ½ cup (1 stick) salted butter, melted, plus extra for greasing
- ¾ cup confectioners' sugar
- 1 teaspoon lemon juice

1. Preheat the oven to 400°F. Grease the sections of a madeleine pan with melted butter and sprinkle with a little flour, shaking the pan so the flour coats the sections. Tap out any excess flour.

2. Crush the cardamom pods with a mortar and pestle and lift out the shells. Pound the seeds again to break them up. Put the eggs and sugar in a heatproof bowl with the orange zest and cardamom seeds and whisk over a saucepan of simmering water until the mixture is thick and pale and the whisk leaves a trail when lifted from the bowl.

3. Sift the flour and baking powder into the bowl and fold in gently with a large metal spoon. Once the flour is mostly combined, drizzle the butter around the edges of the mixture and stir in gently. Spoon into the pan sections until about two-thirds full.

4. Bake in the preheated oven for 12–15 minutes or until slightly risen and just firm to the touch. Transfer the madeleines to a wire rack to cool while you clean the pan and bake a second batch.

5. Beat the confectioners' sugar in a small bowl with the lemon juice and enough of the orange juice to produce a consistency that thinly coats the back of the spoon. Spoon the icing over the madeleines and let set.

VANILLA COOKIES

MAKES ABOUT 20

- 2½ cups all-purpose flour, plus extra for dusting
- I cup (2 sticks) unsalted butter, cut into small pieces, plus extra for greasing
- I cup confectioners' sugar
- 2 egg yolks
- 2 teaspoons vanilla extract

1. Put the flour in a food processor and add the butter. Process until the mixture resembles fine bread crumbs.

2. Add the sugar, egg yolks, and vanilla extract and process to a smooth dough. Wrap and chill for at least 30 minutes before using.

3. Meanwhile, preheat the oven to 350°F and lightly grease two cookie sheets.

4. Roll out the dough on a lightly floured surface and, using cookie cutters, cut out shapes. Place them on the prepared cookie sheets, spaced slightly apart, and bake in the preheated oven for 15 minutes or until pale golden. Let sit on the cookie sheets to slightly harden, then transfer to a wire rack to cool completely.

TIP

- For chocolate cookies, replace ¼ cup of the flour with ⅓ cup of unsweetened cocoa powder.

SPICY GINGERBREAD

MAKES ABOUT 24 COOKIES
- ½ cup (1 stick) unsalted butter, softened, plus extra for greasing
- ½ cup firmly packed light brown sugar
- 1 egg, beaten
- ⅓ cup molasses
- 3 cups all-purpose flour, plus extra for dusting
- 1 tablespoon baking powder
- 1½ teaspoons ground ginger

1. Beat together the butter and sugar until creamy. Stir in the egg and molasses. Sift the flour, baking powder, and ginger into the bowl and stir in with a wooden spoon to form a stiff dough.

2. Turn out the dough onto a lightly floured surface and knead lightly until smooth. Wrap and chill for at least 30 minutes before using.

3. Meanwhile, preheat the oven to 350°F and lightly grease two cookie sheets.

4. Roll out the dough on a lightly floured surface and, using cookie cutters, cut out shapes. Place on the prepared cookie sheets, spaced slightly apart, and bake in the preheated oven for 15 minutes or until the dough has risen slightly and is beginning to darken around the edges. Let sit on the cookie sheets for a few minutes to slightly harden, then transfer to a wire rack to cool completely.

SPICY BUTTERMILK COOKIES

MAKES 20

- 6 tablespoons butter, softened, plus extra for greasing
- ¾ cup granulated sugar
- ⅔ cup buttermilk
- 1¾ cups all-purpose flour
- ½ teaspoon baking soda
- 2 teaspoons ground allspice

1. Preheat the oven to 400°F and lightly grease two cookie sheets.

2. Cream together the butter and sugar in a bowl until light and fluffy. Beat in the buttermilk. Sift the flour, baking soda, and spice into the bowl and beat into the creamed mixture.

3. Drop rounded tablespoons of the dough onto the prepared cookie sheets, spacing them well apart because the cookies will almost double in size.

4. Bake in the preheated oven for 10–15 minutes until golden. Let sit on the cookie sheets for a few minutes to slightly harden, then transfer to a wire rack to cool completely.

MALTED DROP COOKIES

MAKES 18
- ½ cup (1 stick) butter, softened
- ½ cup granulated sugar
- 1 egg, lightly beaten
- 1 teaspoon vanilla extract
- ⅓ cup chocolate malt powder
- ½ cup all-purpose flour
- ½ cup rolled oats

1. Preheat the oven to 375°F and line two cookie sheets with parchment paper.

2. Cream together the butter and sugar until light and fluffy. Beat in the egg and vanilla extract. Sift together the chocolate malt powder and flour into the bowl and beat into the creamed mixture along with the oats until all the ingredients are well combined.

3. Drop heaping teaspoons of the dough onto the prepared cookie sheets, spacing well apart. Bake in the center of the preheated oven for 10–12 minutes, until just golden. The lower cookie sheet may need slightly longer. Let sit on the cookie sheets for a few minutes to slightly harden, then transfer to a wire rack to cool completely.

PEANUT BUTTER COOKIES P56

FRUITY & NUTTY

RICCIARELLE COOKIES

These Italian cookies are a favorite at Christmas. Their main ingredients are grown in the fertile areas round the hills of Tuscany.

MAKES ABOUT 14-16

- 1¼ cups superfine sugar
- 2 cups ground almonds
- Finely grated zest of 2 lemons
- ½ teaspoon baking powder
- 2 egg whites
- Confectioners' sugar, for dusting

1. Preheat the oven to 350°F and line two cookie sheets with parchment paper.

2. Mix together the sugar, almonds, lemon zest, and baking powder in a large bowl. Lightly whisk the egg whites in a separate bowl, then add to the dry ingredients and mix to a thick dough.

3. Transfer the dough to a work surface dusted with plenty of confectioners' sugar. Cut the dough in half and shape each piece into a log about 8 inches long. Cut across into ½-inch slices and space the pieces slightly apart on the prepared cookie sheets.

4. Bake in the preheated oven for about 15 minutes, until the cookies have risen slightly and are just beginning to brown; they'll still be soft to touch. Let sit on the cookie sheets for a few minutes to slightly harden, then transfer to a wire rack and dust generously with confectioners' sugar. Let cool completely.

PISTACHIO COOKIES

- -

MAKES 20
- ¾ cup shelled pistachio nuts
- ¾ cup all-purpose flour
- ¾ teaspoon baking powder
- ½ cup (1 stick) salted butter, cut into pieces, plus extra for greasing
- ½ cup superfine sugar
- Confectioners' sugar, for dusting

1. Preheat the oven to 325°F and lightly grease a large cookie sheet.

2. Put the nuts in a heatproof bowl and cover with boiling water. Let sit for 1 minute, then drain and rinse in cold water.

3. Transfer onto several thicknesses of paper towels and rub with additional layers of paper towels to remove the skin. Peel away the skins that are clinging to the nuts. (Skinning the nuts is not essential but it gives the cookies a more vibrant color.) Finely chop the nuts in a food processor and transfer to a plate.

4. Add the flour, baking powder, and butter to the processor and blend until the mixture resembles coarse bread crumbs. Briefly blend in the superfine sugar, then add the nuts and mix until binding together.

5. Transfer onto a work surface and shape into an 8-inch-long log. Cut into 20 slices and roll into balls. Space well apart on the prepared cookie sheet and flatten slightly.

6. Bake in the preheated oven for 12–15 minutes, until the cookies have spread and are just turning pale golden around the edges. Let sit on the cookie sheet for a few minutes to slightly harden, then transfer to a wire rack to cool completely. Serve lightly dusted with confectioners' sugar.

FRUIT & NUT COOKIES

MAKES 12
- Butter, for greasing
- I quantity Chunky Oat Cookie dough (see page 37)
- ⅓ cup mixed dried small berries, such as cranberries, blueberries, currants, and strawberries
- 4 candied cherries, chopped
- I tablespoon pumpkin seeds
- 2 tablespoons slivered almonds

1. Preheat the oven to 350°F and lightly grease a large cookie sheet.

2. Shape the cookie dough into 12 balls and flatten each until about 3½ inches in diameter. Place on the prepared cookie sheet, spacing them well apart.

3. Sprinkle the dried fruit in a circle around the edges of the cookies, then top the dried fruit with the cherries, pumpkin seeds, and slivered almonds to make a garland. Bake in the preheated oven for 15 minutes or until risen and pale golden. Let sit for on the cookie sheet for a few minutes to slightly harden, then transfer to a wire rack to cool completely.

FRENCH HONEY & FRUIT COOKIES

MAKES ABOUT 12

- ⅓ cup candied or crystallized fruit, finely chopped
- 1 tablespoon rum
- Butter, for greasing
- 1 quantity Vanilla Cookie dough (see page 40)
- 3–4 tablespoons thick honey
- Sifted confectioners' sugar, for dusting

1. Soak the fruit in the rum for at least 30 minutes. Meanwhile, preheat the oven to 375°F and lightly grease a cookie sheet.

2. Roll out the dough, sprinkle with the fruit, fold it up, and knead lightly until the fruit is well mixed into the dough. Roll out thinly and cut into 2-inch circles.

3. Place the circles on the prepared cookie sheet and bake in the preheated oven for 10–12 minutes, until set and golden. Let sit on the cookie sheet for a few minutes to slightly harden, then transfer to a wire rack to cool completely. Sandwich together pairs of the cookies with the honey. To serve, dust lightly with sifted confectioners' sugar.

WALNUTS BARQUETTES

MAKES 14

Pâte sucrée
- 1 cup all-purpose flour
- 4 tablespoons butter, softened
- ¼ cup superfine sugar
- 2 egg yolks
- Few drops of vanilla extract

Walnut filling
- 4 tablespoons butter
- ¼ cup superfine sugar
- 1 egg, beaten
- 3 tablespoons all-purpose flour, sifted
- ⅔ cup ground walnuts

Icing
- 1 cup confectioners' sugar, sifted
- 1 egg white

1. To make the pâte sucrée, sift the flour onto a large board, make a well in the center, and put the butter, superfine sugar, egg yolks, and vanilla extract into the well. Using the fingertips of one hand, work these ingredients together until well blended, then draw in the flour. Knead lightly until smooth and chill for 1 hour.

2. Roll out the dough thinly and use to line 14 barquette molds. Prick and chill for 20 minutes. Preheat the oven to 375°F.

3. To make the walnut filling, cream together the butter and sugar until light and fluffy, then add the egg and flour and beat well. Fold in the walnuts. Spoon the mixture into a pastry bag fitted with a plain tip and pipe into the chilled pastry shells.

4. To make the icing, mix the confectioners' sugar with the egg white until smooth. Spoon into a pastry bag fitted with a fine tip for writing and pipe a crisscross pattern over each of the barquettes.

5. Bake in the preheated oven for 20 minutes. Let sit in the molds for 5 minutes, then transfer to a wire rack to cool completely.

PECAN MERINGUE CRISPS

These crunchy fingers are best enjoyed with a coffee for a sweet snack that is very quick and simple to make.

MAKES 22-24
- 1 cup pecans
- 2 egg whites
- ½ cup firmly packed light brown sugar
- 1 teaspoon vanilla extract
- Confectioners' sugar, for dusting

1. Preheat the oven to 325°F and line a large cookie sheet with parchment paper.

2. Blend the nuts in a food processor until finely ground.

3. Whisk the egg whites in a thoroughly clean bowl until forming peaks. Gradually whisk in the sugar, a tablespoonful at a time, and whisking well after each addition until the meringue is thick and glossy. Sprinkle with the ground pecans and vanilla extract and stir in, using a large metal spoon.

4. Put the batter in a large pastry bag fitted with a ¾-inch plain tip and pipe lines about 3 inches long onto the prepared cookie sheet, spacing them slightly apart.

5. Bake in the preheated oven for 20 minutes or until nearly firm. Let sit on the cookie sheet for a few minutes to slightly harden, then transfer to a wire rack to cool completely. Dust generously with confectioner's sugar.

ALMOND BUTTER
COOKIES

- -

MAKES ABOUT 36
- 1⅓ cups all-purpose flour
- ½ teaspoon baking powder
- ½ cup (1 stick) butter or margarine, softened, plus extra for greasing
- ⅓ cup superfine sugar
- ½ teaspoon vanilla extract
- 2 tablespoons water

Praline
- ⅔ cup superfine sugar
- ¼ cup almonds

1. Preheat the oven to 325°F and lightly grease three cookie sheets.

2. To make the praline, put the sugar and almonds in a small, heavy saucepan over medium-high heat and stir occasionally until the sugar dissolves and turns a pale amber.

3. Pour out the caramel mixture onto a greased and lined cookie sheet to make a layer ¼ inch thick and spread with a greased spatula. Set aside until cold.

4. Break the praline into pieces and put them into a plastic bag. Crush the pieces coarsely with a rolling pin.

5. To make the cookies, sift the flour and baking powder into a bowl and set aside. Put the butter and sugar into a large bowl and cream until light and fluffy. Add the vanilla extract and mix well. Add the flour mixture alternately with the water, mixing until smooth after each addition. Stir the crushed praline into the dough.

6. Drop rounded teaspoonfuls, 2 inches apart, onto the prepared cookie sheets. Bake in the preheated oven for 14–16 minutes or until the edges are lightly browned. Let sit on the cookie sheets for a few minutes to slightly harden, then transfer to a wire rack to cool completely.

PECAN SNAPS

MAKES ABOUT 30 SMALL OR 8-10 LARGE

- 4 tablespoons butter, plus extra for greasing
- ¼ cup firmly packed light brown sugar
- 3 tablespoons light corn syrup
- ⅓ cup all-purpose flour, plus extra for dusting
- ¼ cup pecans, finely chopped
- I teaspoon vanilla extract

1. Preheat the oven to 350°F. Grease and lightly flour two cookie sheets.

2. Melt the butter in a medium saucepan over gentle heat. Stir in the sugar and the corn syrup. Increase the heat to high and bring the mixture to a boil, stirring constantly, until the sugar has dissolved. Remove the pan from the heat. Stir in the flour and pecans until well combined. Blend in the vanilla extract.

3. Place rounded spoonfuls of the dough onto the prepared cookie sheets about 2 inches apart. For "curls," drop teaspoonfuls on the cookie sheets; to make "tulips," drop tablespoonfuls on the sheets, 3 inches apart. Using a small spatula spread the mixture into an even circle.

4. Bake in the preheated oven for 6-8 minutes for small cookies and 8-10 minutes for large ones, or until browned. When cool enough to handle, bend into the desired shape. If the cookies become too cool to shape, return them to the oven briefly to soften.

PEANUT BUTTER COOKIES

MAKES 32

- ½ cup (1 stick) unsalted butter, at room temperature, plus extra for greasing
- ⅔ cup light brown sugar
- ½ cup chunky peanut butter
- 1 egg, lightly beaten
- 1¼ cups all-purpose flour
- ½ teaspoon baking powder
- ¾ cup unsalted peanuts

1. Preheat the oven to 375°F and lightly grease three large cookie sheets.

2. Beat the butter and sugar together in a mixing bowl or a food processor until pale and creamy. Add the peanut butter, egg, flour, and baking powder and stir together until combined. Stir in the peanuts.

3. Drop large teaspoonfuls of the dough onto the prepared cookie sheets, leaving 2-inch gaps between each for them to spread during cooking. Flatten the mounds slightly and bake in the preheated oven for 12 minutes, until golden around the edges.

4. Let sit on the cookie sheets for a few minutes to slightly harden, then transfer to a wire rack to cool completely.

TIP

• For peanut butter & chocolate chip cookies, use only ⅓ cup unsalted peanuts and add 2 oz milk chocolate chips. Then make and bake the cookies as above.

GOLDEN RAISIN & CARAWAY COOKIES

MAKES 14

- 1⅔ cups all-purpose flour, plus extra for dusting
- 1 teaspoon baking powder
- 1 teaspoon caraway seed, roughly crushed
- Grated zest of ½ lemon
- ⅓ cup superfine sugar, plus extra for sprinkling
- 6 tablespoons butter, diced, plus extra for greasing
- ⅓ cup golden raisins
- 1 egg, beaten
- 1–2 tablespoons low-fat milk

1. Preheat the oven to 350°F and lightly grease a cookie sheet.

2. Mix the flour and baking powder together into a mixing bowl or food processor, then add the crushed seed, lemon zest, and sugar. Add the butter and rub in with your fingertips or process until the mixture resembles fine bread crumbs.

3. Stir in the golden raisins, then the egg and enough milk to mix to a soft but not sticky dough.

4. Knead lightly, then roll out on a lightly floured surface until ¼ inch thick. Stamp out 3-inch circles using a fluted round cookie cutter. Transfer to the prepared cookie sheet. Reknead the scraps and continue rolling and stamping out until all the dough has been used.

5. Prick the cookies with a fork, then sprinkle with a little extra sugar and bake in the preheated oven for 8–10 minutes, until pale golden. Let sit on the cookie sheet for a few minutes to slightly harden, then transfer to a wire rack to cool completely.

TIP

- For fennel & orange cookies, replace the caraway seed and lemon zest in the recipe above with 1 teaspoon roughly crushed fennel seeds and the grated zest of ½ a small orange. Continue the recipe as above.

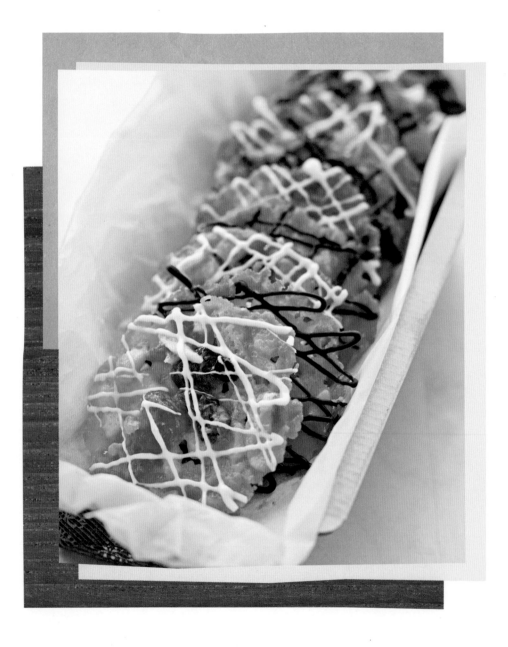

FLORENTINES

MAKES 48

- ⅔ cup (1¼ sticks) unsalted butter, plus extra for greasing
- ¾ cup superfine sugar
- ¼ cup heavy cream
- ⅓ cup chopped candied peel
- ¼ cup candied cherries, chopped
- ½ cup slivered almonds
- ⅓ cup dried cranberries
- 3 tablespoons pine nuts
- ⅓ cup all-purpose flour
- 5 oz semisweet chocolate
- 5 oz white chocolate

1. Preheat the oven to 350°F and lightly grease two large cookie sheets and line with parchment paper.

2. Put the butter and sugar in a saucepan and heat gently until the butter is melted. Increase the heat and bring the mixture to a boil. Immediately remove the saucepan from the heat, add the cream, fruits, nuts and flour, and stir well until evenly combined.

3. Drop 12 heaping teaspoonfuls of the dough onto the prepared cookie sheets, leaving a 2-inch gap for spreading. Bake in the preheated oven for 7 minutes.

4. Remove the cookie sheets from the oven and, using a 3-inch cookie cutter, carefully drag the edges of the cookies into neat circles so that they are about 2 inches across. Bake for another 3–4 minutes, until golden around the edges.

5. Remove from the oven and let sit on the cookies sheets for a few minutes to slightly harden, then transfer to parchment paper over a wire rack and let cool completely. Repeat with the remaining dough.

6. Melt the semisweet chocolate and white chocolate in separate bowls set over gently simmering water (do not let the bottoms of the bowls touch the water). Stir until the chocolates are smooth. Spoon the melted chocolates into separate paper pastry bags and drizzle back and forth over the cookies. Let set.

VANILLA & PEANUT WHOOPIES

MAKES 12-14

- 1⅓ cups all-purpose flour, sifted, plus extra for dusting
- 1¼ teaspoons baking powder
- ¼ teaspoon baking soda
- ½ cup superfine sugar
- 2 tablespoons vanilla sugar
- 1 egg
- 3 tablespoons vegetable oil
- 1 tablespoon milk

Filling
- ⅓ cup smooth peanut butter
- 2 tablespoons salted butter, softened, plus extra for greasing
- 3 tablespoons confectioners' sugar, sifted
- 1 teaspoon hot water

1. Preheat the oven to 400°F and lightly grease a large cookie sheet.

2. Put the flour, baking powder, baking soda, and sugars in a bowl. Beat the egg with the vegetable oil and milk and add to the dry ingredients. Beat together to form a thick paste, adding a little more milk if the mixture feels crumbly.

3. Roll teaspoonfuls of the dough into balls about the size of a cherry, using floured hands. Space well apart on the prepared cookie sheet and flatten slightly.

4. Bake in the preheated oven for 12 minutes, until the cookies have spread and are pale golden. Let sit on the cookie sheet for a few minutes to slightly harden, then transfer to a wire rack to cool completely.

5. Make the filling by beating together the peanut butter, butter, and confectioners' sugar until smooth. Add the measured hot water and beat until light and fluffy. Use to sandwich together pairs of the cookies.

ALMOND & WHITE CHOCOLATE KISSES

MAKES 18
- ⅔ cup blanched almonds
- ½ cup (1 stick) unsalted butter, softened, plus extra for greasing
- ½ cup superfine sugar
- ¾ cup all-purpose flour, plus extra for dusting
- ¼ teaspoon baking powder

Filling
- 4 oz white chocolate, chopped
- 2 tablespoons unsalted butter

1. Preheat the oven to 350°F and lightly grease two cookie sheets.

2. Put the almonds in a food processor and blend until finely ground. Add the butter and sugar, sift in the flour and baking powder, and blend until the mixture starts to come together.

3. Turn out onto a lightly floured surface and pat into a smooth dough. Roll small balls of the dough, about the size of a cherry and space on the prepared cookie sheets.

4. Bake in the preheated oven for about 15 minutes, until risen, cracked, and pale golden. Let sit on the cookie sheets for a few minutes to slightly harden, then transfer to a wire rack to cool completely.

5. Make the chocolate filling by melting the chocolate and butter in a saucepan. Use to sandwich together the macaroons in pairs.

TIP

- For gluten-free almond macaroons, grease and line a large cookie sheet with nonstick parchment paper. Whisk 2 egg whites until forming peaks and gradually whisk in ½ cup superfine sugar. Stir in 1¼ cups ground almonds. Place heaping teaspoonfuls, spaced slightly apart, on the prepared cookie sheet and press a blanched almond onto the top of each. Bake as above.

BANANA WALNUT COOKIES

This classic combination is a healthy and low G.I. option. A well-mashed banana is key to making the dough cook evenly.

MAKES 20
- 1¾ cups all-purpose flour
- 1 teaspoon baking powder
- ½ cup (1 stick) butter, cut into cubes, plus extra for greasing
- ¾ cup firmly packed light brown sugar
- ¾ cup coarsely chopped walnuts
- 2 small or 1 large banana, peeled
- 1 egg
- ¼ cup milk

1. Preheat the oven to 350°F and lightly grease two cookie sheets.

2. Sift the flour and baking powder into a bowl. Add the butter and blend with your fingertips until the mixture resembles fine bread crumbs. Stir in the sugar and walnuts.

3. Mash the banana with a fork and beat in the egg. Stir in the milk. Add to the bowl and mix until well combined.

4. Drop spoonfuls of the dough onto the prepared cookie sheets, spacing well apart. Bake in the preheated oven for about 15 minutes until golden. Let sit on the cookie sheets for a few minutes to slightly harden, then transfer to a wire rack to cool completely.

LEMON MACADAMIA NUT COOKIES

MAKES 24

- ½ cup (1 stick) butter, softened, plus extra for greasing
- ½ cup superfine sugar
- 2 egg yolks
- Grated zest of ½ lemon
- ¼ cup lemon juice
- 1¾ cups all-purpose flour
- ⅓ cup cornstarch
- ¾ cup macadamia nuts, lightly chopped

1. Preheat the oven to 375°F and lightly grease two cookie sheets.

2. Cream together the butter and sugar until light and fluffy. Beat in the egg yolks, lemon zest, and juice.

3. Sift the flour and cornstarch and beat into the mixture. Add the nuts and stir until well mixed.

4. Drop heaping tablespoons of the dough onto the prepared cookie sheets and flatten slightly with the back of a spoon. Bake in the preheated oven for 10–12 minutes, until golden. Let sit on the cookie sheets for a few minutes to slightly harden, then transfer to a wire rack to cool completely.

COCONUT
GEMS

MAKES 24

- ½ cup (1 stick) butter, softened, plus extra for greasing
- ¾ cup confectioners' sugar, plus extra for dusting
- 1 egg
- 1 teaspoon vanilla extract
- 1 cup all-purpose flour
- ½ teaspoon baking powder
- 1 cup shredded dried coconut

1. Preheat the oven to 350°F and lightly grease two cookie sheets. Put all the ingredients in a bowl and beat until mixed to a smooth, thick dough.

2. Place rounded teaspoonfuls of the dough on the prepared cookie sheets, spacing them well apart. Bake in the preheated oven for about 15 minutes or until the cookies have spread and the edges are just beginning to brown. Let sit on the cookie sheets for a few minutes to slightly harden, then transfer to a wire rack to cool completely.

3. Serve dusted with confectioners' sugar.

ORANGE & PEANUT BUTTER COOKIES

MAKES 10-12

- 1 cup (2 sticks) butter, softened, plus extra for greasing
- ¾ cup superfine sugar
- ¾ cup firmly packed light brown sugar
- 2 eggs
- 1 teaspoon vanilla extract
- 2 cups all-purpose flour
- 1 teaspoon baking soda
- 1 cup semisweet or milk chocolate chips
- ⅔ cup mixed nuts (walnuts, pecans, almonds, hazelnuts, etc.), chopped

1. Preheat the oven to 325°F and lightly grease two cookie sheets.

2. Cream together the butter and sugars until light and fluffy. Beat in the eggs and vanilla extract. Sift the flour with the baking soda and beat into the mixture. Add the chocolate chips and nuts and stir until well combined.

3. Drop large rounded tablespoons of the dough onto the prepared cookie sheets, five or six per sheet, well spaced as the cookies will spread.

4. Bake in the preheated oven for 15–18 minutes, until golden. Let sit on the cookie sheets for a few minutes to slightly harden, then transfer to a wire rack to cool completely.

CARAMELITAS

MAKES 20

- 2¼ cups rolled oats
- 1⅔ cups all-purpose flour
- 1 teaspoon baking soda
- 1½ cups firmly packed light brown sugar
- ½ teaspoon salt
- 1 cup (2 sticks) unsalted butter, melted
- 10 oz semisweet chocolate, coarsely chopped
- 1 cup pecans, lightly toasted and coarsely chopped
- 1 cup caramel sauce (or dulce de leche)

1. Preheat the oven to 350°F and line the bottom of a shallow 12-inch square baking pan with parchment paper.

2. Put the oats, flour, baking soda, sugar, and salt into a bowl and mix together. Add the butter and mix well.

3. Spread half of the batter in the bottom of the prepared pan. Press out evenly using the back of a spoon. Bake in the preheated oven for 10 minutes.

4. Remove and sprinkle the chocolate and nuts evenly over the surface. Drizzle the caramel sauce evenly over the top. Sprinkle the reserved oat batter on top and press gently with the back of a spoon.

5. Return to the oven for 20–25 minutes, until golden brown. Let cool in the pan completely and cut into bars to serve.

FIG &
DATE ROLLS

- -

MAKES 24

Filling
- 1½ cups finely chopped dried figs
- ½ cup finely chopped pitted dates
- ½ cup water
- Finely grated zest of 1 lemon
- ½ cup superfine sugar

Dough
- ½ cup (1 stick) butter
- ⅓ cup superfine sugar
- 1 teaspoon ground cinnamon
- 1 egg
- ¾ cup ground almonds
- 1¾ cups all-purpose flour

1. To make the filling, put all the ingredients into a saucepan and stir over gentle heat until the sugar is dissolved. Let simmer, uncovered, for about 15 minutes, until the mixture is thick and pulpy. Let cool.

2. To make the dough, beat together the butter, sugar, cinnamon, and egg. Stir in the ground almonds and flour. Knead lightly and divide into four. Wrap each portion in plastic wrap and chill for 30 minutes.

3. Preheat the oven to 350°F. Roll out each portion of dough between sheets of parchment paper to 4 x 8 inches. Spread one-quarter of the filling along each rectangle, leaving a ½-inch border. Fold the long sides over the filling to meet in the center and press gently together. Tuck the ends under.

4. Place the rolls, seam side down, on nonstick cookie sheets. Bake in the preheated oven for 20–25 minutes, until lightly browned. Remove and let cool completely, then cut into slices.

WALNUT KISSES

MAKES 40
- ½ cup walnuts
- ¾ cup confectioners' sugar
- 2 egg whites

1. Preheat the oven to 300°F and line two cookie sheets with sheets of parchment paper.

2. Process the walnuts in a food processor until finely ground. Sift the confectioners' sugar into a bowl.

3. Put the egg whites in a large, grease-free mixing bowl and beat until frothy. Gradually add the confectioners' sugar and beat until combined. Place the bowl over a saucepan of gently simmering water and beat until the mixture is thick and stands in stiff peaks. Remove from the saucepan and beat until cold.

4. Carefully fold in the ground walnuts until just blended, then spoon into a pastry bag fitted with a large plain or star tip. Pipe small rosettes or balls slightly spaced onto the prepared cookie sheets.

5. Bake in the preheated oven for about 30 minutes, until the cookies can be easily removed from the paper. Let cool completely.

CHOCOLATE & CHILE COOKIES P81

CHOCOLATE
COOKIES

CHOCOLATE BROWNIE COOKIES

MAKES ABOUT 30

- 7 oz semisweet chocolate, broken into pieces
- 4 tablespoons salted butter
- 2 eggs
- ¾ cup firmly packed light brown sugar
- 1 teaspoon vanilla extract
- 1⅓ cups all-purpose flour
- ½ teaspoon baking soda
- Confectioners' sugar, for dusting

1. Preheat the oven to 325°F and line two large cookie sheets with baking parchment. Sprinkle plenty of confectioners' sugar into a plate.

2. Put the chocolate and butter into a heatproof bowl and melt in the microwave or over a saucepan of simmering water (do not let the bottom of the bowl touch the water). Stir frequently and remove from the heat once the chocolate has almost melted. Let cool slightly.

3. Whisk the eggs, sugar, and vanilla extract in a bowl until smooth. Add the flour, baking soda, and chocolate mixture and mix to a smooth dough.

4. Once the chocolate mixture is cool enough to handle, roll into balls about the size of a large truffle. Roll in the confectioners' sugar and space about 2 inches apart on the prepared cookie sheets. Flatten slightly.

5. Bake in the preheated oven for about 10 minutes, until risen and cracked. They should still feel soft. Let sit on the cookie sheets for a few minutes to slightly harden, then transfer to a wire rack to cool completely and dust with extra icing sugar.

CHOCOLATE MARYLAND COOKIES

- - - - - - - - - - - - - - -

MAKES 20-22

- ¾ cup (1½ sticks) salted butter, softened, plus extra for greasing
- ½ cup superfine sugar
- ¼ cup light corn syrup
- 2 cups all-purpose flour
- ½ cup semisweet or milk chocolate chips, or chopped chocolate

1. Preheat the oven to 375°F and lightly grease two cookie sheets.

2. Put the butter, sugar, and corn syrup in a bowl and beat together until smooth.

3. Add the flour and chocolate and mix the ingredients until they bind together to make a dough.

4. Roll heaping teaspoonfuls of the dough into balls and space them well apart on the prepared cookie sheets. Flatten slightly and bake in the preheated oven for 15 minutes, until pale golden. Let sit on the cookie sheets for a few minutes to slightly harden, then transfer to a wire rack to cool completely.

CHUNKY CHOCOLATE COOKIES

MAKES 24

- 4 tablespoons salted butter, softened, plus extra for greasing
- ⅔ cup firmly packed light brown sugar
- 1 egg, beaten
- ⅔ cup all-purpose flour
- ½ teaspoon baking powder
- ¾ cup rolled oats
- ⅓ cup raisins, chopped
- 7 oz semisweet or milk chocolate, chopped

1. Preheat the oven to 350°F and lightly grease two cookie sheets.

2. Put the butter and sugar in a bowl and beat to a smooth thick paste. Beat in the egg. Add the flour, baking powder, oats, and raisins and mix well until the ingredients are evenly combined.

3. Spoon heaping teaspoonfuls of the dough onto the prepared cookie sheets, spacing them well apart. Bake in the preheated oven for 15–20 minutes or until the cookies have spread and are pale golden. Let sit on the cookie sheets for a few minutes to slightly harden, then transfer to a wire rack to cool completely.

4. Melt the chocolate in a heatproof bowl set over a saucepan of simmering water (make sure the bottom of the bowl does not touch the water) or in short spurts in the microwave. Spread thinly over the flat side of each cookie and let set.

CHOCOLATE CINNAMON CRUNCHIES

- - - - - - - - - - - - - - - - - - - -

MAKES 36
- 2 cups all-purpose flour
- 2 teaspoons baking soda
- 1 teaspoon ground cinnamon
- ¼ teaspoon salt
- ½ cup (1 stick) butter or margarine, softened
- ¼ cup vegetable shortening
- 1⅓ cups superfine sugar
- ½ teaspoon vanilla extract
- 1 egg
- 3 tablespoons light corn syrup
- 2 oz semisweet chocolate, melted and cooled

1. Preheat the oven to 350°F.

2. Sift the flour, baking soda, cinnamon, and salt into a bowl, then set aside.

3. In a large bowl, beat together the butter or margerine and shortening. Add a generous 1 cup of the sugar and beat until fluffy. Add the vanilla extract, then the egg, beating well. Blend in the corn syrup and chocolate. Gradually work in the dry ingredients, beating until just well combined.

4. Spread the remaining sugar in a shallow pan. Shape the dough into balls about 1½ inches in diameter. Place the balls, six to eight at a time, in the pan and roll in the sugar to coat them lightly all over. Place the balls about 2 inches apart on ungreased cookie sheets.

5. Bake in the preheated oven for about 15 minutes or until the cookies feel firm when touched lightly. Let sit on the cookie sheets for a few minutes to slightly harden, then transfer to a wire rack to cool completely.

WHITE CHOCOLATE & LEMONGRASS COOKIES

MAKES 16-18

- 7 oz white chocolate, chopped
- 1 stalk lemongrass
- 1⅓ cups flour
- 2 teaspoons baking powder
- 6 tablespoons unsalted butter, diced, plus extra for greasing
- ⅓ cup golden raisins
- 1 egg, beaten

1. Preheat the oven to 400°F and grease a large cookie sheet.

2. Melt 5 oz of the chocolate in a small heatproof bowl in a microwave oven using short spurts or set over a saucepan of simmering water (make sure the bottom of the bowl does not touch the water).

3. Bruise the lemongrass by tapping it firmly with a rolling pin. Slice the lemongrass and blend in a food processor until finely chopped. Add the flour, baking powder, and butter and blend until the mixture resembles fine bread crumbs.

4. Add the melted chocolate, golden raisins, and egg and blend lightly until the dough binds together. Turn the dough onto the work surface and shape into a log, about 9 inches long. Cut into chunky slices and place on the prepared cookie sheet, spacing the pieces slightly apart and reshaping them if squashed.

5. Bake in the preheated oven for about 15 minutes, until risen and pale golden. Let sit on the cookie sheet for a few minutes to slightly harden, then transfer to a wire rack to cool completely.

6. Melt the remaining chocolate as in step 1 above and put in a paper pastry bag. Snip off the tip and drizzle the chocolate over the cookies to decorate.

RED VELVET COOKIES

- -

MAKES 20

- 4 tablespoons salted butter, softened, plus extra for greasing
- ¾ cup superfine sugar
- 1¼ cups all-purpose flour
- 2 tablespoons unsweetened cocoa powder
- 1¼ teaspoons baking powder
- ½ teaspoon baking soda
- 1 egg
- 1 small beet, finely grated
- ½ teaspoon vanilla extract
- Few drops red food coloring, optional
- 3 oz white chocolate, chopped

Filling

- 1 cup cream cheese
- ¼ cup confectioners' sugar

1. Put the butter and sugar in a bowl and beat together until smooth. Sift in the flour, cocoa powder, baking powder, and baking soda.

2. Add the egg, beet, vanilla extract, and red food coloring, if using. Mix well to make a firm dough. Shape into a log 12 inches long and chill for at least 1 hour or until firm.

3. Preheat the oven to 375°F and lightly grease two cookie sheets. Cut the cookie log into thin slices and space slightly apart on the prepared cookie sheets. Bake in the preheated oven for 12–15 minutes, until the cookies have spread slightly and are beginning to turn darker around the edges. Let sit on the cookie sheets for a few minutes to slightly harden, then transfer to a wire rack to cool completely.

4. Beat the cream cheese in a bowl with the confectioners' sugar until smooth and spreadable. Use to sandwich together the cookies.

5. Melt the chocolate in a heatproof bowl in a microwave oven using short spurts or set over a saucepan of simmering water. Use a teaspoon or pastry bag to drizzle lines of chocolate over the cookies. Let set.

TRIPLE CHOCOLATE COOKIES

MAKES 20

- 6 tablespoons butter, at room temperature, plus extra for greasing
- ¾ cup firmly packed light brown sugar
- 1 egg
- 1¼ cups all-purpose flour
- 1¼ teaspoons baking powder
- 2 tablespoons unsweetened cocoa powder
- 4 oz white chocolate, chopped
- 4 oz milk chocolate, chopped

1. Preheat the oven and lightly grease two cookie sheets.

2. Beat together the butter and sugar in a mixing bowl until pale and creamy. Stir in the egg, flour, baking powder, and cocoa powder and mix until smooth.

3. Stir in the chopped chocolate, then spoon 20 mounds of the dough onto the prepared cookie sheets, leaving space between for them to spread during cooking.

4. Bake in the preheated oven for 8–10 minutes, until lightly browned. Let sit on the cookie sheets for a few minutes to slightly harden, then transfer to a wire rack to cool completely.

5. These are best eaten on the day they are made.

TIP

- For chocolate, vanilla, & hazelnut cookies, follow the basic recipe above but omit the cocoa powder and increase the quantity of all-purpose flour to 1⅓ cups. Omit the white chocolate and add ½ cup coarsely chopped hazelnuts and 1 teaspoon vanilla extract in its place.

CHOCOLATE & CHILE COOKIES

MAKES 12

- ¾ cup all-purpose flour
- 1 tablespoon unsweetened cocoa powder
- 1 teaspoon baking powder
- ½ teaspoon baking soda
- ½ teaspoon ground cinnamon
- ¼ cup firmly packed light brown sugar
- 4 tablespoons butter, diced, plus extra for greasing
- ¼ teaspoon chopped chile from a jar or mild freshly chopped red chile
- 2 tablespoons light corn syrup
- 4 oz semisweet chocolate, finely chopped

1. Preheat the oven to 350°F and lightly grease two cookies.

2. Stir all the dry ingredients together in a bowl or a food processor. Add the butter and chile and rub in with your fingertips or process until the mixture resembles fine bread crumbs.

3. Add the corn syrup, then mix together first with a spoon and then squeeze the crumbs together with your hands to form a ball. Knead in the chopped chocolate, then shape the dough into a log and slice into 12.

4. Roll each piece into a ball and arrange on the prepared cookie sheets. Cook one cookie sheet at a time in the center of the preheated oven for 8–10 minutes, until browned and the tops are craggy. Let sit on the cookie sheets for a few minutes to slightly harden, then transfer to a wire rack to cool completely.

5. These cookies are best eaten on the day they are made and delicious served while still warm.

TIP

- For chocolate and ginger cookies, make the cookies in the same way as above but use 2 tablespoons chopped candied ginger instead of the chile and ground cinnamon.

CHOCOLATE JUMBLE CRUNCHES

MAKES 24

- 9 oz semisweet chocolate, broken into pieces
- ½ cup (1 stick) lightly salted butter
- 3 oz chocolate honeycomb toffee (sponge candy) bars
- 10 graham crackers
- ½ cup walnut pieces
- 4 oz white chocolate, chopped

1. Melt the semisweet chocolate and butter in a large mixing bowl and let cool. Break the candy bars and crackers into small pieces.

2. Stir the honeycomb, crackers, and walnuts into the melted chocolate until evenly combined. Add the white chocolate to the bowl and fold in gently.

3. Put the mixture onto a large sheet of parchment paper, spreading it into a log shape about 14 inches long.

4. Bring the paper up over the mixture on the long sides and squeeze the ends of the paper together so that the mixture is compacted into a long log shape. Twist the ends of the paper like a candy wrapper and chill for at least 2 hours or until set.

5. Peel away the paper and cut the log into ½-inch slices. (If the log is too brittle to slice, let it sit at room temperature for a while to soften slightly.)

TIP

- Use almost any other nuts that you prefer (or have in the cupboard). Hazelnuts, almonds, and Brazil nuts are all suitable alternatives. You can also try adding raisins, if desired.

CHOCOLATE BUTTER COOKIES

MAKES 36

- 2 cups all-purpose flour, plus extra for dusting
- ¼ cup unsweetened cocoa powder
- Pinch of salt
- ¾ cup plus 2 tablespoons (1¾ sticks) chilled unsalted butter, diced, plus extra for greasing
- ¾ cup confectioners' sugar
- 2 egg yolks
- 1 teaspoon vanilla extract

1. Sift the flour, cocoa powder, and salt into a food processor, add the butter, and process until the mixture resembles fine bread crumbs. Add the sugar and pulse briefly, then add the egg yolks and vanilla extract and process until the mixture just starts to come together.

2. Transfer the dough to a work surface and shape into a circle. Wrap in plastic wrap and chill for 30 minutes.

3. Preheat the oven to 400°F and lightly grease three large cookie sheets.

4. Roll out the dough on a lightly floured surface to ¼ inch thick. Use a 3-inch cookie cutter to stamp out circles and put them on the prepared cookie sheets.

5. Bake in the preheated oven for around 8–10 minutes, until lightly golden around the edges. Let sit on the cookie sheets for a few minutes to slightly harden, then transfer to a wire rack to cool completely.

TIP

- For plain cookies, increase the flour to 2¼ cups and omit the cocoa powder.

CHOCOLATE KISSES

MAKES ABOUT 25
- 2 large egg whites
- ¼ teaspoon cream of tartar
- 1 cup plus 2 tablespoons superfine sugar
- ¼ cup unsweetened cocoa powder, sifted
- 1½ cups ground almonds
- 1 teaspoon almond extract

Filling
- 4 oz semisweet chocolate, chopped
- ½ cup heavy cream

1. Preheat the oven to 300°F and line two large cookie sheets with parchment paper.

2. Whisk the egg whites and cream of tartar in a clean bowl until stiff, then gradually whisk in the sugar, 1 tablespoon at a time, until the mixture thickens. Fold in the cocoa powder, ground almonds, and almond extract with a metal spoon until evenly combined.

3. Spoon the mixture into a pastry bag fitted with a large star tip and pipe 1-inch rosettes onto the prepared cookie sheets (you should have about 40–50 rosettes, depending on the size).

4. Bake in the preheated oven for 15 minutes, until the cookies are just set. Remove from the oven and let cool completely on the cookie sheets.

5. To make the filling, put the chocolate and cream in a bowl set over a saucepan of gently simmering water (do not let the bottom of the bowl touch the water). Heat gently, stirring until the chocolate is melted. Cool and then chill for 30 minutes.

6. Whip the chocolate mixture until thick and fluffy and use to sandwich together the cookies to make kisses.

MINT CHOCOLATE SANDWICHES

MAKES 24-28
- 1 quantity Chocolate Butter Cookie dough (see page 84)
- All-purpose flour, for dusting

Filling
- 5 tablespoons unsalted butter, softened, plus extra for greasing
- 1¼ cups confectioners' sugar, sifted
- 1 teaspoon peppermint extract

Icing
- 8 oz semisweet chocolate

1. Preheat the oven to 400°F and lightly grease three large cookie sheets.

2. Make up the cookie dough according to the recipe on page 84. Roll out the dough on a lightly floured surface until ⅛ inch thick. Use a 2-inch plain cookie cutter to stamp out circles. Put them on the prepared cookie sheets and bake in the preheated oven for 10 minutes, until starting to brown around the edges. Let sit on the cookie sheets for a few minutes to slightly harden, then transfer to a wire rack to cool completely.

3. To make the filling, put the butter, confectioners' sugar, and peppermint extract in a bowl and, using an electric hand mixer, beat together until smooth. Use the filling to sandwich together the cookies.

4. For the icing, put the chocolate in a heatproof bowl set over a saucepan of gently simmering water (do not let the bottom of the bowl touch the water) and stir until melted. One at a time, put a cookie on a fork and dip it into the melted chocolate, then place on a sheet of parchment paper to set. Repeat with the remaining cookies.

CARAMEL PINE NUT SLICES

MAKES 8

- ½ cup (1 stick) unsalted butter, softened, plus extra for greasing
- ⅓ cup superfine sugar
- 1 cup all-purpose flour, plus extra for dusting
- ⅓ cup plus 1 tablespoon rice flour
- Pinch of salt
- 7 oz semisweet chocolate

Pine nut caramel
- 4 tablespoons unsalted butter
- ¼ cup firmly packed light brown sugar
- 1 (14-oz) can sweetened condensed milk
- ⅓ cup pine nuts

1. Put the butter and sugar in a bowl and, using an electric hand mixer, beat together until pale and light. Sift in the flour, rice flour, and salt and work the ingredients together to form a soft dough. Shape the dough into a flat circle, wrap in plastic wrap, and chill for 30 minutes.

2. Preheat the oven to 375°F. Grease an 8-inch square baking pan and line it with parchment, letting the paper overhang the sides of the pan.

3. Roll out the dough on a lightly floured surface and press into the prepared pan, smoothing it as flat as possible. Bake in the preheated oven for 20–25 minutes, until golden. Remove from the oven and let cool.

4. To make the pine nut caramel, put the butter, sugar, and condensed milk into a saucepan and heat gently, stirring constantly, until the butter has melted and the sugar has completely dissolved. Increase the heat and bring to a boil, whisking constantly for up to 5 minutes, until the mixture thickens. Remove from the heat, stir in the pine nuts, and pour the mixture over the shortbread layer. Let sit until set. Chill for 2 hours until really firm.

5. Put the chocolate in a heatproof bowl set over a saucepan of gently simmering water (do not let the bottom of the bowl touch the water), stirring until melted. Pour the melted chocolate over the caramel layer and spread flat with a spatula. Let set, remove from the pan, and cut into slices.

CHOCOLATE REFRIGERATOR BARS

MAKES 30 SLICES

- 1 lb semisweet chocolate, broken into pieces
- ½ cup (1 stick) unsalted butter, plus extra for greasing
- 1 cup coarsely crushed graham crackers
- ½ cup coarsely chopped dried figs
- ½ cup dried cranberries
- ⅓ cup hazelnuts, toasted
- ⅓ cup almonds, toasted and coarsely chopped
- Confectioners' sugar, for dusting (optional)

1. Grease a 7 x 9-inch rectangular cake pan and line the bottom with parchment paper.

2. Put the chocolate and butter into a heatproof bowl set over a saucepan of gently simmering water (do not let the bottom of the bowl touch the water) and stir over low heat until melted. Stir in all the remaining ingredients.

3. Spoon the batter into the prepared pan. Press well into the bottom and sides of the pan and smooth the surface with a spatula.

4. Cover with aluminium foil and chill for 4 hours or overnight.

5. Carefully work around the edges of the cake with the spatula and unmold onto a board, removing the paper from the bottom. Dust with confectioners' sugar, if desired, and serve in thin slices.

TIP

- Spray a 9 x 5 x 3-inch loaf pan with spray olive oil and line with parchment paper. For white chocolate rocky road, put 12 oz white chocolate, broken up, in a heatproof bowl set over a saucepan of simmering water (do not let the bowl touch the water) and heat to melt. Stir 7 oz coarsely chopped Turkish delight (or another gelatin-based chocolate bar), ½ cup shelled pistachio nuts, and ⅓ cup shredded dried coconut into the chocolate. Pour the mixture into the pan and chill for 4 hours. Turn out, remove the paper, and slice.

CHOCOLATE CHIP COOKIES WITH GINGER

MAKES 40
- ½ cup (1 stick) unsalted butter, softened, plus extra for greasing
- ½ cup superfine sugar
- ½ cup firmly packed light brown sugar
- 2 eggs, lightly beaten
- 1⅔ cups all-purpose flour
- 1½ teaspoons baking powder
- Heaping ½ cup chocolate chips
- ⅔ cup finely chopped crystallized (candied) ginger

1. Preheat the oven to 375°F and lightly grease two cookie sheets.

2. Put the butter and sugars in a bowl and, using an electric hand mixer, beat together until light and fluffy. Gradually beat in the eggs, a little at a time, beating well after each addition, until the mixture becomes creamy. Stir in the flour and baking powder and fold in the chocolate chips and ginger to make a soft, sticky dough.

3. Drop teaspoonfuls of the dough, spaced well apart onto the prepared cookie sheets and bake in the preheated oven for 10–12 minutes, until lightly golden. Let sit on the cookie sheets for a few minutes to slightly harden, then transfer to a wire rack to cool completely. Repeat with the remaining dough to make 40 cookies.

CHOCOLATE MACAROONS

MAKES ABOUT 25

- 2 oz rum-flavored or semisweet chocolate
- 2 egg whites
- ½ cup superfine sugar
- 1¼ cups ground almonds
- About 25 chocolate-coated coffee beans, to decorate

1. Line a large cookie sheet with parchment paper. Grate the chocolate.

2. Whisk the egg whites until stiff. Gradually whisk in the sugar until the mixture is thick and glossy. Gently fold in the ground almonds and grated chocolate. Put the batter into a large pastry bag fitted with a large plain tip and pipe small circles, about 1½ inches in diameter, onto the prepared cookie sheet. Alternatively, place small teaspoonfuls on the cookie sheet.

3. Press a chocolate-coated coffee bean into the center of each macaroon. Bake in the preheated oven for about 15 minutes, until slightly risen and just firm. Let the macaroons sit on the paper to cool.

TIP

- Chocolate-coated coffee beans are available from some supermarkets and specialty coffee stores. If you can't find a supplier, decorate each cookie with a whole blanched almond.

CHOCOLATE SPICE COOKIES

Rich and spicy, these cookies are delicious served with a strong pot of coffee for a mid-morning break.

MAKES 20
- 5 oz rum-flavored, semisweet, or milk chocolate
- 1¾ cups all-purpose flour, plus extra for dusting
- 1 teaspoon ground allspice
- ½ cup (1 stick) firm butter or margarine, plus extra for greasing
- ⅔ cup firmly packed light brown sugar
- 1 egg
- 1 egg yolk
- ½ cup mixed dried fruit

1. Preheat the oven to 350°F and lightly grease a large cookie sheet. Finely chop the chocolate.

2. Put the flour and spice in a food processor. Add the butter or margarine, cut into small pieces, and blend until the mixture resembles bread crumbs. Blend in the sugar, egg, egg yolk, dried fruit, and chocolate until the mixture starts to bind together.

3. Turn out the dough onto a floured surface and knead lightly. Roll out to a thickness of ¼ inch and cut out 20 circles, using a 3-inch cookie cutter. Place the circles on the prepared cookie sheet.

4. Bake in the preheated oven for 12–15 minutes, until starting to color around the edges. Let sit on the cookie sheets for a few minutes to slightly harden, then transfer to a wire rack to cool completely.

GLAZED CHOCOLATE GINGER HEARTS

MAKES 25

- ½ cup (1 stick) unsalted butter, softened, plus extra for greasing
- ⅔ cup superfine sugar
- 1 egg
- ⅓ cup molasses
- 3¼ cups all-purpose flour
- 1 tablespoon baking powder
- 2 teaspoons ground ginger

To decorate
- 7 oz rum-flavored or semisweet chocolate, broken into pieces
- 7 oz milk chocolate, broken into pieces
- 1½ oz white chocolate disks

1. Beat together the butter and sugar until pale and creamy. Add the egg and molasses, sift the flour, baking powder, and ginger into the bowl, and mix the ingredients together making a dough. Knead lightly and chill for 30 minutes.

2. Preheat the oven to 350°F and lightly grease two cookie sheets. Roll out the dough to a thickness of ¼ inch and cut out heart shapes, using a cookie cutter. Transfer the shapes to the prepared cookie sheets, spacing them slightly apart. Reroll the scraps to make more cookies.

3. Bake in the preheated oven for about 10 minutes, until slightly risen. Let sit on the cookie sheets for a few minutes to slightly harden, then transfer to a wire rack to cool completely. Melt the rum-flavored or semisweet chocolate and milk chocolate in two separate heatproof bowls set over saucepans of simmering heat (make sure the bowls do not touch the water).

4. Using a tablespoon, spoon the rum-flavored or semisweet chocolate over about half the cookies, reserving a little for decoration. Lay a white chocolate disk in the center of half the coated cookies. Use the milk chocolate to cover the remaining cookies, again reserving a little and laying a white chocolate disk in the center of half the coated cookies.

5. Put the reserved milk chocolate in a pastry bag fitted with a fine tip and pipe wavy lines over the edges of the chocolate disks on the rum-flavored or semisweet chocolate-covered cookies. Use the reserved rum-flavored or semisweet chocolate to decorate the cookies covered with milk chocolate and the chocolate disks. Let set.

FROSTED CHOCOLATE WHOOPIES

MAKES 12-14

- 1¼ cups all-purpose flour, plus extra for dusting
- 1¼ teaspoons baking powder
- ¼ teaspoon baking soda
- ¼ teaspoon unsweetened cocoa powder
- ½ cup superfine sugar
- 2 tablespoons vanilla sugar
- 1 egg
- 3 tablespoons vegetable oil
- 1 tablespoon milk
- 2 oz semisweet or milk chocolate, chopped

Filling
- ½ cup cream cheese
- 2 tablespoons confectioners' sugar, sifted
- 1 teaspoon finely grated orange zest
- Few drops of orange extract (optional)

1. Lightly grease a cookie sheet and preheat the oven to 400°F. Put the flour, baking powder, baking soda, cocoa powder, and sugars in a bowl. Beat the egg with the vegetable oil and milk and add to the dry ingredients. Beat together to form a thick dough, adding a little more milk if the mixture feels crumbly.

2. Take teaspoonfuls of the dough and roll into balls, about the size of a cherry, using floured hands. Space well apart on the prepared cookie sheet and flatten slightly.

3. Bake in the preheated oven for 12 minutes, until the dough has spread and is pale golden. Let sit on the cookie sheets for a few minutes to slightly harden, then transfer to a wire rack to cool completely.

4. Make the filling by beating together the cream cheese, confectioners' sugar, orange zest, and extract, if using. Use to sandwich the cookies together. Melt the chocolate by putting it in a heatproof bowl over simmering water (do not let the bottom of the bowl touch the water) or in a microwave oven using short spurts, and spread over the tops of the whoopies.

CHOCOLATE CIGARS

MAKES 16
- 1 egg white
- ¼ cup superfine sugar
- 2 tablespoons all-purpose flour
- 1 tablespoon unsweetened cocoa powder
- 2 tablespoons heavy cream
- 2 tablespoons unsalted butter, melted
- 5 oz rum-flavored or semisweet chocolate, broken into pieces

1. Preheat the oven to 425°F and line four cookie sheets with parchment paper.

2. Beat together the egg white and sugar until blended. Sift the flour and cocoa powder into the bowl. Stir in the cream and butter.

3. Place four heaping spoonfuls of the dough, spaced well apart, on one of the prepared cookie sheets and spread lightly with the back of a spoon. Bake in the preheated oven for 4 minutes, until the cookies have spread and the edges are beginning to darken.

4. Remove from the oven and let sit for 30 seconds. Using a spatula, lift each cookie from the paper and wrap them around the handles of wooden spoons until set into shape. Carefully twist the cookies off the spoons and transfer to a wire rack to cool completely. Repeat with the remaining dough on the remaining cookie sheets.

5. Melt the chocolate in a heatproof bowl set over a saucepan of simmering water (do not let the bottom of the bowl touch the water) or in a microwave using short spurts, and dip one side of each cookie into it, letting the excess chocolate fall back into the bowl. Let the cookies sit on a sheet of wax paper until set.

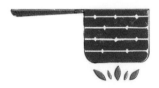

CHOCOLATE RING COOKIES

MAKES 16

- Butter, for greasing
- 1 quantity Chunky Oat Cookie dough, chilled (see page 37)
- Flour, for dusting
- 4 oz white chocolate, broken into pieces
- 3 oz bittersweet chocolate, in a block
- ½ cup unblanched hazelnuts, coarsely chopped
- crystallized rose petals

1. Preheat the oven to 350°F and lightly grease two cookie sheets.

2. Roll out the cookie dough on a lightly floured surface, and cut out circles using a 3¾-inch plain or fluted round cookie cutter. Using a 1¼-inch round cutter, cut out the centers to make rings. Place on the prepared cookie sheets, spacing them slightly apart, and reroll the scraps to make extras.

3. Bake in the preheated oven for 15 minutes or until beginning to darken around the edges. Let sit on the cookie sheets for a few minutes to slightly harden, then transfer to a wire rack to cool completely.

4. Melt the white chocolate in a heatproof bowl set over a saucepan of simmering water (do not let the bottom of the bowl touch the water) or in a microwave oven using short spurts. Using a potato peeler, pare off curls from the bittersweet chocolate.

5. Using a teaspoon, drizzle a little white chocolate over one cookie and sprinkle with some hazelnuts, rose petals, and chocolate curls. Repeat with the other cookies. Let sit in a cool place to set for about 1 hour.

TRIPLE CHOCOLATE BISCOTTI

MAKES ABOUT 28

- Butter, for greasing
- 1 quantity Biscotti dough (see page 35)
- Flour, for dusting
- ½ cup milk chocolate chips
- 5 oz bittersweet chocolate, broken into pieces
- 2 oz white chocolate, broken into pieces

1. Preheat the oven to 325°F and lightly grease a large cookie sheet.

2. Turn out the dough onto a lightly floured surface and gently work in the chocolate chips until evenly combined. Divide the mixture in half and shape each into a log about 9 inches long. Place on the prepared cookie sheet, spacing them well apart, and flatten slightly.

3. Bake in the preheated oven for 30 minutes or until risen and just firm. Let sit on the cookie sheet to cool for 15 minutes, then transfer to a board and, using a serrated knife, cut across into ½-inch-thick slices.

4. Arrange on the prepared cookie sheet, cut sides down, and bake for an additional 15 minutes, until crisp. Let sit on the cookie sheets for a few minutes to slightly harden, then transfer to a wire rack to cool completely.

5. Line a baking pan or clean cookie sheet with parchment paper. Melt the bittersweet and white chocolates in two separate heatproof bowls set over saucepans of simmering water (do not let the bottom of the bowls touch the water). Dip about one-third of each biscotti in the bittersweet chocolate, letting the excess fall back into the bowl. Place each cookie on the parchment paper.

6. Using a teaspoon, drizzle thin lines of white chocolate back and forth over the bittersweet chocolate to decorate. Let sit in a cool place to set for about 1 hour.

CHOCOLATE FLORENTINES

MAKES 14

- 4 tablespoons unsalted butter, plus extra for greasing
- ¼ cup light brown sugar
- 1 tablespoon heavy cream
- ⅓ cup pistachio nuts, skinned and chopped
- ½ cup slivered almonds
- 3 tablespoons candied cherries, chopped
- 3 tablespoons raisins
- 2 tablespoons all-purpose flour
- Vegetable oil, for greasing
- 3 oz bittersweet chocolate, broken into pieces
- 3 oz milk chocolate, broken into pieces

1. Preheat the oven to 350°F and lightly grease two cookie sheets.

2. Melt the butter in a saucepan and stir in the sugar until dissolved. Bring to a boil, then remove from the heat. Stir in the cream, pistachio nuts, almonds, cherries, raisins, and flour and mix well.

3. Place heaping teaspoonfuls of the dough on the prepared cookie sheets, spacing them well apart. Bake in the preheated oven for 8–10 minutes, swapping the sheets over halfway through, until the cookies are golden, bubbling, and spreading.

4. Grease a round cookie cutter with the vegetable oil. Remove the cookies from the oven and, using the prepared cookie cutter, push the edges of each cookie into the center to create a neat round edge. Return to the oven for 2 minutes. Let sit on the cookie sheets for a few minutes to slightly harden, then transfer to a wire rack to cool completely.

5. Line a cookie sheet with wax paper. Melt the chocolates in two separate heatproof bowls set over saucepans of simmering water (do not let the bottom of the bowls touch the water). Dip the edges of the cookies in the chocolate—half in bittersweet, half in milk—and let sit on the wax paper in a cool place to set for about 1 hour.

LITTLE DINOS P107

DECORATED COOKIES

PINK CHAMPAGNE
COCKTAILS

- - - - - - - - - - - - - -

MAKES 16

- ¾ cup plus 2 tablespoons (1¾ sticks) chilled unsalted butter, diced, plus extra for greasing
- 2¼ cups all-purpose flour, plus extra for dusting
- ¾ cup confectioners' sugar
- 2 egg yolks
- 2 teaspoons vanilla extract

Buttercream
- 1 cup confectioners' sugar, sifted
- 5 tablespoons unsalted butter, softened
- A few drops of pink liquid or paste food coloring

To decorate
- Sugar sprinkles
- Pink-tinted silver balls

1. Put the butter and flour in a food processor and blend until the mixture resembles bread crumbs. Add the sugar, egg yolks, and vanilla extract and blend until the mixture comes together to form a smooth dough. Wrap in plastic wrap and chill for at least 1 hour.

2. Trace and cut out a cocktail glass shape from a picture that is about 4 x 3¼ inches to use as a template. Preheat the oven to 350°F and lightly grease two cookie sheets.

3. Roll out the cookie dough on a lightly floured surface. Lay the template over the dough and, using a small, sharp knife, cut around it. Place on the prepared cookie sheets, spacing them slightly apart, and reroll the scraps to make 16 in all.

4. Bake in the preheated oven for 15 minutes, or until pale golden. Let sit on the cookie sheets for a few minutes to slightly harden, then transfer to a wire rack to completely cool. Meanwhile, put the sugar and butter into a bowl and beat until smooth. Beat the food coloring into the buttercream and put half in a pastry bag fitted with a fine plain tip.

5. Spread a little frosting across the center of the cookies so they look like half-filled glasses. Pipe an outline of frosting around the cookie edges. Sprinkle the glass cavity area with sugar sprinkles. Pipe frosting dots for the bubbles and sprinkle with the pink-tinted silver balls.

3D WINTER WONDERLAND

- -

MAKES 20 COOKIES

- ½ cup (1 stick) butter, at room temperature, plus extra for greasing
- ½ cup superfine sugar
- 2 egg yolks
- 1 tablespoon unsweetened cocoa powder
- 1 teaspoon ground cinnamon
- 1 ⅓ cups all-purpose flour

Icing
- 1¼ cups confectioners' sugar, sifted
- 4–5 teaspoons egg white or water

1. Beat together the butter and sugar in a mixing bowl until pale and creamy. Stir in the egg yolks, cocoa powder, and cinnamon, then gradually mix in the flour to form a smooth soft dough. Chill for 15 minutes.

2. Preheat the oven to 350°F and lightly grease two cookie sheets.

3. Roll out the dough between two sheets of parchment paper until ¼ inch thick. Stamp out festive shapes using cookie cutters about 3 inches in diameter. Transfer to the prepared cookie sheets. Reknead the scraps and continue rolling and stamping out until all the dough has been used. Make a small hole in each cookie, using the handle of a teaspoon.

4. Bake in the preheated oven for 10–12 minutes, until lightly browned. Remake the hole in each cookie, then let cool on the cookie sheets.

5. Mix the confectioners' sugar and egg white or water to a smooth thick icing. Spoon into a parchment paper pastry bag, snip off the tip, and pipe lines, dots, and swirls to decorate the cookies. Let harden.

6. Thread the fine ribbon through the holes and hang on the Christmas tree or on white painted twigs standing in a pitcher.

TIP

- For orange & allspice hearts, follow the recipe above but omit the cocoa powder, add an extra tablespoon of flour, and stir in the grated zest of 1 small orange. Replace the ground cinnamon with 1 teaspoon ground allspice. Cut out heart-shape cookies from the dough, make ribbon holes in them, bake, and decorate as above.

CHRISTMAS BAUBLES

MAKES 20

- Butter, for greasing
- I quantity Vanilla Cookie dough, chilled (see page 40)
- Flour, for dusting
- Fine ribbon, for threading

To decorate

- 2 tablespoons egg white
- A few drops each of orange and green liquid or paste food colorings (or colors of your choice)
- White sugar sprinkles
- I quantity Royal Icing (see page 10)

1. Preheat the oven to 350°F and lightly grease two cookie sheets.

2. Roll out the cookie dough on a lightly floured surface and, using a 3½-inch round cookie cutter, cut out circles. Place on the prepared cookie sheets, spacing them slightly apart, and reroll the scraps to make extras.

3. Using a toothpick, make a small hole about ½ inch from the edge of each circle for threading the ribbon. Bake in the preheated oven for 15 minutes or until pale golden. Remove from the oven and immediately remake the holes, because the dough will have risen slightly during baking. Transfer to a wire rack to cool completely.

4. Beat the egg white to break it up and divide between two small dishes. Add the orange coloring to one and the green to the other. Use a fine paintbrush to paint designs over each cookie, then sprinkle with sugar sprinkles.

5. Put the royal icing into a pastry bag fitted with a small star tip. Pipe a line of icing between the sugars and around the edges of the cookies to finish.

6. Let sit in a cool place to set for at least 1 hour before threading with ribbon for hanging.

SHOOTING STARS

- - - - - - - - - - - - - - - - - -

MAKES 24

- ¾ cup plus 2 tablespoons (1¾ sticks) chilled unsalted butter, diced, plus extra for greasing
- 2¼ cups all-purpose flour, sifted, plus extra for dusting
- ½ cup firmly packed light brown sugar
- 2 teaspoons ground ginger
- 2 egg yolks
- 2 teaspoons vanilla extract

To decorate
- 1 ⅔ cups confectioners' sugar
- About 5 teaspoons cold water
- A few drops each of orange and yellow liquid or paste food colorings
- Edible gold food coloring

1. Put the flour and butter in a food processor and blend until the mixture resembles bread crumbs. Add the sugar, ground ginger, egg yolks, and vanilla extract and blend to make a smooth dough. Wrap in plastic wrap and chill for at least 1 hour.

2. Preheat the oven to 350°F and lightly grease two cookie sheets.

3. Roll out the dough on a lightly floured surface and cut out shooting star-shape cookies using a cookie cutter. Place on the prepared cookie sheets, spacing them slightly apart, and reroll the scraps to make 24 in total.

4. Bake in the preheated oven for 15 minutes or until the dough has risen slightly and is beginning to darken. Let sit on the cookie sheets for a few minutes to slightly harden, then transfer to a wire rack to cool completely.

5. Put the confectioners' sugar in a bowl and beat in enough cold water to make a thick but smooth icing. Divide the icing between two bowls and color one orange and one yellow. Place in two separate pastry bags fitted with fine tips (or use paper pastry bags and snip off the tips).

6. Pipe star-shape outlines and broken lines of piping on the tails of the stars. Let sit in a cool place to set for about 30 minutes. Use the gold food coloring to paint highlights over the cookies.

LITTLE DINOS

MAKES 20

- ¾ cup plus 2 tablespoons (1¾ sticks) chilled unsalted butter, diced, plus extra for greasing
- 2¼ cups all-purpose flour, plus extra for dusting
- ¾ cup confectioners' sugar, plus extra for dusting
- 2 egg yolks
- 2 teaspoons vanilla extract
- 10 oz green ready-to-use fondant
- 4 oz yellow ready-to-use fondant
- 2¾ oz white chocolate rainbow disks
- 1 oz brown ready-to-use fondant
- 1 quantity Quick Buttercream, to decorate (see page 10)

1. Put the butter and flour into a food processor and blend until the mixture resembles bread crumbs. Add the sugar, egg yolks, and vanilla and blend to a smooth dough. Wrap in plastic wrap and chill for 1 hour.

2. Preheat the oven to 350°F and lightly grease two cookie sheets. Roll out the dough on a lightly floured surface and cut out circles with a 4-inch cutter, rerolling the scraps to make 20 circles. Cut each circle in half and bake on the prepared cookie sheets in the preheated oven for 15 minutes, until pale golden. Let sit on the cookie sheets for a few minutes to slightly harden, then transfer to a wire rack to completely cool.

3. Knead the green fondant a little on a surface dusted with confectioners' sugar. Tear the yellow fondant into pieces and dot over the green fondant. Roll the lump of fondant with your hands into a thick log. Fold in half and roll again. Repeat rolling and folding until the colors have marbled together.

4. Put the buttercream in a pastry bag with a fine plain tip. Roll out the marbled fondant thinly. Lay a cookie over the fondant and, using a sharp knife, cut around it, adding a fondant tail: Pipe buttercream over and lay the marbled icing on top. Repeat with the rest of the cookies. Reroll the fondant scraps and cut out heads, marking the mouths. Secure to the bodies with buttercream. Shape and secure ears and feet. Cut the chocolate disks into triangles and, using buttercream, secure along the top of each "body," making the triangles smaller at the tails. Pipe eyes and claws with buttercream. Shape and secure balls of brown fondant for pupils.

BABY SHOWER COOKIES

MAKES 20

- Butter, for greasing
- I quantity Vanilla Cookie dough, chilled (see page 40)
- Flour, for dusting

To decorate
- I quantity Royal Icing (see page 10)
- 5 pink jelly beans, halved lengthwise
- 3 oz pale blue, pink, or yellow ready-to-use fondant
- 10 small blue, pink, or yellow ribbon bows

1. Copy the bootie and bottle shapes on the opposite page to make simple templates. Preheat the oven to 350°F and grease two cookie sheets.

2. Roll out the cookie dough thinly on a lightly floured surface. Lay the templates over the dough and, using a small, sharp knife, cut around them. Place on the prepared cookie sheets, spacing them slightly apart, and reroll the scraps to make 20 in all. Bake in the preheated oven for 15 minutes, or until pale golden. Let sit on the cookie sheets for a few minutes to slightly harden, then transfer to a wire rack to completely cool.

3. Place a little of the royal icing in a pastry bag fitted with a fine plain tip. Add a few drops of water to the remaining icing until the icing forms a flat surface when left to stand for 15 seconds.

4. Pipe a line of icing around the edges of the cookies. Pipe a line of circles across the ankles of the booties and a diagonal line of piping across the center of the bottles. Using a small teaspoon, drizzle a little of the thinned icing onto the lower part of the bottles, spreading it to the edges with the back of a teaspoon and easing it into the corners with a toothpick. Spread the icing onto the bootie-shape cookies in the same way, easing it around the piping across the ankles.

5. Secure a jelly bean half, cut side down, to the top of each bottle with a little icing. Shape a little band of ready-to-use fondant and secure around the neck of the bottles. Let sit for 30 minutes. Pipe white decorative lines and secure bows with dots of icing to finish the booties and pipe ready-to-use fondant on the bottles. Let set again for 30 minutes.

WISE OLD OWLS

MAKES 18
- Butter, for greasing
- 1 quantity Vanilla Cookie dough, chilled (see page 40)
- Flour, for dusting
- 1 tablespoon egg white, lightly beaten
- 2 teaspoons unsweetened cocoa powder
- 1 teaspoon water
- 1¼ cups confectioners' sugar, sifted

To decorate
- 2 oz each of white, blue, and yellow ready-to-use fondant

1. Draw a simple owl picture, trace the outline and cut out to make a template about 2 inches high. Preheat the oven to 350°F and lightly grease two cookie sheets.

2. Roll out the cookie dough on a lightly floured surface. Lay the template over the dough and, using a small, sharp knife, cut around it. Reroll the scraps to make 18 in all. Place on the prepared cookie sheets, spacing them apart.

3. Beat together the egg white, cocoa powder, and measured water to make a smooth, thin paste. Using a fine paintbrush, paint the wing, head, and beak areas on the owls.

4. Bake in the preheated oven for 15 minutes, or until pale golden. Let sit on the cookie sheets for a few minutes to slightly harden, then transfer to a wire rack to completely cool.

5. Beat the confectioners' sugar with enough water to make a consistency that holds its shape. Put the icing into a pastry bag fitted with a fine plain tip. Use the white ready-to-use fondant to shape eyes, then secure them with a little icing from the bag. Use the blue fondant to shape centers for the eyes, then secure with icing. Cut out feet in yellow fondant and secure. Use the icing left in the bag to paint the wing and breast feathers. Let sit in a cool place to set for about 1 hour.

CARS

- - - - - - - - - - - - - -

MAKES 14-16

- Butter, for greasing
- 1 quantity Vanilla Cookie dough, chilled (see page 40)
- Flour, for dusting

To decorate
- 4 oz white ready-to-use fondant
- Confectioners' sugar, for dusting
- 1 tube yellow decorator icing
- Double quantity Quick Buttercream (see page 10)
- A few drops of blue liquid or paste food coloring
- Large round candies for wheels
- A selection of small candies

1. Draw or copy an outline of a bubble car about 3–4 inches long and cut it out to use as a template. Preheat the oven to 350°F and lightly grease two cookie sheets.

2. Roll out the cookie dough on a lightly floured surface. Lay the template over the dough and, using a small, sharp knife, cut around it. Place the shapes on the prepared cookie sheets, spacing them slightly apart, and reroll the scraps to make extras.

3. Bake in the preheated oven for 15 minutes or until pale golden. Let sit on the cookie sheets for a few minutes to slightly harden, then transfer to a wire rack to completely cool.

4. Thinly roll out the white fondant on a surface lightly dusted with confectioners' sugar and cut out small window shapes. Secure in place on the car shapes with a little decorator icing from the tube. Use more decorator icing to pipe outlines around the cookies.

5. Color the buttercream with the food coloring and put it in a pastry bag fitted with a star tip. Use the frosting to pipe circles for wheel tires and outlines around the windows.

6. Press the candies in place for wheels and finish decorating the cars with smaller candies. Pipe lines of yellow icing over the wheel candies to represent spokes.

LACY
BUTTERFLIES

MAKES 16
- Butter, for greasing
- 1 quantity Vanilla Cookie dough, chilled (see page 40)
- Flour, for dusting

To decorate
- 1 quantity Royal Icing (see page 10)
- A few drops each of green and lilac liquid food coloring
- 2 tubes of pastel-colored glitter icing in contrasting shades

1. Draw and cut out butterfly shapes about 2 inches big to use as a template. Preheat the oven to 350°F and lightly grease two cookie sheets.

2. Roll out the cookie dough on a lightly floured surface. Lay the template over the dough and, using a small, sharp knife, cut around it. Place on the prepared cookie sheets, spacing them apart, and reroll the scraps to make extras.

3. Bake in the preheated oven for 15 minutes or until pale golden. Let sit on the cookie sheets for a few minutes to slightly harden, then transfer to a wire rack to completely cool.

4. Put a little of the royal icing in a pastry bag fitted with a fine writer tip. Divide the remaining icing between two bowls. Add a few drops of green food coloring to one bowl and lilac to the other. Carefully stir a few drops of water into each one until the icing forms a flat surface when left to stand for 15 seconds.

5. Pipe a line of icing down the centers and around the edges of the cookies. Pipe circles of icing in the center of each wing and fill each circle with fine, wavy filigree lines. (These can be irregular shapes as long as they match on the opposite wing.) Using a small teaspoon, drizzle the green icing into the plain areas of half the cookies. Using a toothpick, draw this to the edges at intervals (but don't fill in completely with icing). Repeat with the lilac icing on the remaining cookies.

6. Let sit in a cool place to set for about 1 hour or until the icing is just dry. Pipe a thick band of glitter icing down the center of each butterfly.

BEES & HIVES

- - - - - - - - - - - - - -

MAKES 24

- Butter, for greasing
- 1 quantity Chocolate Cookie dough, chilled (see page 40)
- Flour, for dusting

To decorate

- 4 oz white chocolate, broken up
- 5 oz yellow ready-to-use fondant
- Confectioners' sugar, for dusting
- 4 oz pale brown ready-to-use fondant
- 1 oz white ready-to-use fondant
- Bittersweet chocolate chips
- 2 sheets of rice paper

1. Preheat the oven to 350°F and lightly grease two cookie sheets. Roll out the cookie dough on a lightly floured surface. Cut out twelve 2½-inch circles and place on the cookie sheets, spacing them slightly apart. Cut out 3 x 2-inch rectangles from the remaining dough, then round off one of the ends of each rectangle to make hives. Reroll the scraps for extras.

2. Bake in the preheated oven for 15 minutes or until just beginning to darken around the edges. Let sit on the cookie sheets for a few minutes to slightly harden, then transfer to a wire rack to completely cool. Melt the chocolate in a heatproof bowl set over a saucepan of simmering water (do not let the bowl touch the water) or in a microwave oven with short spurts. Put it in a paper pastry bag and snip off the tip.

3. Roll out the yellow fondant thinly on a surface lightly dusted with confectioners' sugar. Cut out strips, about ¼ inch wide, and lay them across the round cookies, securing with a little piped chocolate. Trim off the excess fondant around the edges of the cookies. Reroll for more strips.

4. Pipe chocolate over the hive cookies in a scribble. Thinly roll out the pale brown fondant and cut into strips. Alternate strips of yellow and pale brown fondant across the cookies. Trim off excess fondant, then cut out a small rectangle from the bottom of each. Use the pale brown fondant scraps to shape and secure the bees' heads. Use the white fondant and chocolate chips to make the eyes. Cut each sheet of rice paper into six and fold the pieces in half lengthwise. Cut out a wing from each piece. Pipe a line of chocolate down their backs and secure the wings. Cool for an hour.

GINGERBREAD NIGHT LIGHTS

MAKES 4
- Flour, for dusting
- 1 quantity Spicy Gingerbread dough, chilled (see page 41)
- 6 oz colored boiled candies
- 1 quantity Royal Icing (see page 10)
- 4 night lights

1. Preheat the oven to 350°F and line two cookie sheets with parchment paper. On a lightly floured surface, thinly roll out half the cookie dough large enough from which to cut out a neat 14 x 7-inch rectangle. Carefully lift onto one prepared cookie sheet and trim the edges to make the rectangle. Using a ruler, cut the dough into eight exact 3½-inch squares.

2. Using a 3½-inch star cutter (measured from point to point), cut out a star shape from each square. The star shapes that you've cut out from the centers can be cooked and decorated separately, if desired. Repeat with the second batch of dough on the second cookie sheet.

3. Bake the squares in the preheated oven for 5 minutes. While they are baking, use a rolling pin or small hammer to lightly crush the candies in their wrappers. Remove the cookie sheets from the oven and sprinkle the crushed candies into the star areas. Return to the oven for an additional 8–10 minutes, until the gingerbread is lightly colored and the candies have melted to fill the stars. (If they haven't completely spread into the corners, use a toothpick to help spread the syrup while it is still soft.) Recut the edges of the cookie squares, because they will have merged together a little during baking, then let sit on the cookie sheets to cool completely.

4. Put the icing in a pastry bag fitted with a fine tip for writing. Pipe a line of icing down one inside edge of four cookies and secure together to make four sides of a box shape. Make three more box shapes. Use the remaining icing to pipe decorative lines around the edges of the boxes. Let set for at least 2 hours. When ready to use, light a night light and lower a gingerbread box over it. (Protect the table with a mat or coaster underneath.)

GINGERBREAD
MEN

MAKES 10-12
- Butter, for greasing
- 1 quantity Spicy Gingerbread dough, chilled (see page 41)
- Flour, for dusting

To decorate
- 1 quantity Quick Buttercream (see page 10)
- 3 oz each of red, orange, yellow, and pink ready-to-use fondant
- Confectioners' sugar, for dusting

1. Preheat the oven to 350°F and lightly grease two cookie sheets.

2. Roll out the cookie dough on a lightly floured surface and, using a gingerbread-man cutter about 5 inches in length, cut out figures in the dough. Place on the prepared cookie sheets, spacing them slightly apart, and reroll the scraps to make extras.

3. Bake in the preheated oven for 15 minutes or until the dough has risen slightly and is beginning to darken around the edges. Let sit on the cookie sheets for a few minutes to slightly harden, then transfer to a wire rack to completely cool.

4. Put the buttercream in a pastry bag fitted with a fine tip for writing (or use a paper pastry bag and snip off the tip). Thinly roll out half of each fondant color on a surface lightly dusted with confectioners' sugar. Using a ¼-½ inch flower plunger cutter, stamp out tiny flower shapes.

5. Reroll the fondant scraps, along with the reserved half of each color, and cut out "shorts" or "sarongs." Position on the cookies, securing them with a little buttercream. Secure garlands of the flowers around the necks of the cookies with buttercream and finish by piping faces with the buttercream and outlining the "shorts" and "sarongs."

SPOTS & STRIPES

MAKES 24

- Butter, for greasing
- 1 quantity Spicy Gingerbread dough, chilled (see page 41)
- Flour, for dusting

To decorate
- 3 oz milk chocolate, broken into pieces
- 4 oz white ready-to-use fondant
- Confectioners' sugar, for dusting
- 2 oz black ready-to-use fondant
- 4 oz chocolate-flavored ready-to-use fondant
- 5 oz yellow ready-to-use fondant
- 2 oz light brown ready-to-use fondant

1. Preheat the oven to 350°F and lightly grease two cookie sheets.

2. Roll out the cookie dough on a lightly floured surface and, using a 3¼-inch round cookie cutter, cut out circles. Place on the prepared cookie sheets, spacing them slightly apart, and reroll the scraps to make extras.

3. Bake in the preheated oven for 15 minutes or until the dough has risen slightly and is beginning to darken around the edges. Let sit on the cookie sheets for a few minutes to slightly harden, then transfer to a wire rack to completely cool. Melt the chocolate in a heatproof bowl set over a saucepan of simmering water (do not let the bowl touch the water).

4. Thinly roll out the white fondant on a surface lightly dusted with confectioners' sugar. Roll thin ropes of the black fondant under the palms of your hands and lay them across the white at slightly irregular intervals. Use the rolling pin to gently roll the black fondant into the white. Using a 2½-inch round cookie cutter, cut out eight circles. Spread one-third of the cookies with a little melted chocolate, then lay the circles of fondant over.

5. Thinly roll out the chocolate-flavored fondant. Use 2 oz of the yellow fondant and the same technique as above to make another eight striped circles. Secure to another eight cookies with melted chocolate.

6. Roll out the remaining yellow fondant. Use the light brown fondant to roll plenty of little balls in various sizes, then sprinkle them over the yellow fondant. Gently roll with the rolling pin. Cut out another eight circles and secure to the remaining cookies with melted chocolate.

FALL COOKIES

MAKES 18-20
- Butter, for greasing
- 1 quantity Vanilla Cookie dough, chilled (see page 40)
- Flour, for dusting

To decorate
- Double quantity Royal Icing (see page 10)
- A few drops each of orange, yellow, and green liquid or paste food colorings

1. Draw pumpkin, acorn, and leaf shapes and trace their outlines. Cut out to make templates. Preheat the oven to 350°F and lightly grease two cookie sheets.

2. Roll out the cookie dough on a lightly floured surface and, using the templates, cut out pumpkin, acorn, and leaf shapes. Place on the prepared cookie sheets, spacing them slightly apart, and reroll the scraps to make extras.Bake in the preheated oven for 15 minutes or until pale golden. Let sit on the cookie sheets for a few minutes to slightly harden, then transfer to a wire rack to completely cool.

3. Spoon a little royal icing into a pastry bag fitted with a fine tip for writing. Divide the remaining icing between three bowls. Beat a food coloring into each bowl of icing, then add a few drops of water to each so that the icing forms a flat surface when left to stand for 15 seconds.

4. Brush the orange icing over the pumpkin shapes, leaving the stems plain. Brush the leaves with the yellow icing, then brush yellow icing over the bottom of the acorns. Brush the top of the acorns with green icing. Pipe a thin line of icing from the fine tip around the cookies to finish and make decorative markings in the centers. Let sit in a cool place to set for about 1 hour.

GHOSTS

MAKES 14-16
- Butter, for greasing
- 1 quantity Vanilla Cookie dough, chilled (see page 40)
- Flour, for dusting

To decorate
- 12 oz white ready-to-use fondant
- ¼ cup confectioners' sugar, plus extra for dusting
- 6 tablespoons orange juice
- 2 oz black ready-to-use fondant

1. Draw ghost shapes on paper and cut out to make two templates. One template should have the eyes and mouth cut out and the other just the ghost outline. Preheat the oven to 350°F and lightly grease two cookie sheets.

2. Roll out the cookie dough on a lightly floured surface. Lay the ghost outline template over the dough and, using a small, sharp knife, cut around it. Place on the prepared cookie sheets, spacing them slightly apart, and reroll the scraps to make extras.

3. Bake in the preheated oven for 15 minutes or until pale golden. Let sit on the cookie sheets for a few minutes to slightly harden, then transfer to a wire rack to completely cool.

4. Thinly roll out the white fondant on a surface lightly dusted with confectioners' sugar. Lay the ghost template with features on the fondant and, using a small, sharp knife, cut around it. Then, using the knife, cut out the eyes and mouth.

5. For a citrus glaze, working quickly, mix together the orange juice and the confectioners' sugar. Spread the cookies with the glaze and gently press the fondant into position. Roll the black fondant into tiny pieces and press into the eye and mouth spaces.

CHRISTMAS TREE DECORATIONS

MAKES 20

- ½ cup (1 stick) butter, at room temperature, plus extra for greasing
- ½ cup superfine sugar
- 2 egg yolks
- 1 tablespoon unsweetened cocoa powder
- 1 teaspoon ground cinnamon
- 1⅓ cups all-purpose flour
- Fine ribbon, for threading

Icing
- 1¼ cups confectioners' sugar, sifted
- 4–5 teaspoons egg white or water

1. Beat together the butter and sugar in a mixing bowl until pale and creamy. Stir in the egg yolks, cocoa powder, and cinnamon, then gradually mix in the flour to form a smooth soft dough. Chill for 15 minutes.

2. Preheat the oven to 350°F and lightly grease two cookie sheets.

3. Roll out the dough between two sheets of parchment paper until ¼ inch thick. Stamp out festive shapes using cookie cutters about 3 inches in diameter. Transfer to the prepared cookie sheets. Reknead the scraps and continue rolling and stamping out until all the dough has been used. Make a small hole in each cookie, using the handle of a teaspoon.

4. Bake in the preheated oven for 10–12 minutes, until lightly browned. Remake the hole in each cookie, then let cool on the cookie sheets.

5. Mix the confectioners' sugar and egg white or water to a smooth thick icing. Spoon into a parchment paper pastry bag, snip off the tip, and pipe lines, dots, and swirls to decorate the cookies. Let harden.

6. Thread the fine ribbons through the holes and hang on the Christmas tree or on white painted twigs standing in a pitcher.

TIP

- For orange and allspice hearts, follow the recipe above but omit the cocoa powder, add an extra tablespoon of flour, and stir in the grated zest of 1 small orange. Replace the ground cinnamon with 1 teaspoon ground allspice. Cut out heart-shape cookies from the dough, make ribbon holes in them, bake, and decorate as above.

OLIVE & PARMESAN GRISSINI, P130

SAVORY COOKIES

BACON, THYME & HERB STICKS

- - - - - - - - - - - - - - - - - - -

MAKES ABOUT 60
- 2 russet potatoes
- 2 oz thinly cut smoked bacon, finely chopped
- ¾ cup all-purpose flour, plus extra for dusting
- 6 tablespoons salted butter, cut into pieces, plus extra for greasing
- ¾ cup shredded cheddar cheese
- 2 teaspoons finely chopped thyme, plus extra to sprinkle
- 1 egg yolk
- Beaten egg, to glaze
- Sea salt, to sprinkle

1. Cut the potatoes into small chunks and cook in boiling salted water until just tender. Drain and return to the saucepan. Mash well and let cool.

2. Cook the bacon in a dry skillet until crisp. Let cool.

3. Put the flour and butter into a food processor and blend until the mixture resembles coarse bread crumbs. Add the cheese, thyme, potatoes, bacon, and egg yolk and blend to a dough. Wrap and chill for at least 3 hours.

4. Preheat the oven to 350°F and lightly grease a large cookie sheet.

5. Roll out the dough on a floured surface to ¼ inch thick and cut into 3½-inch-wide strips. Cut the strips across into thin slices and transfer to the prepared cookie sheet.

6. Brush with beaten egg yolk to glaze. Sprinkle with sea salt and bake in the preheated oven for 20 minutes, until golden. Serve warm or transfer to a wire rack to cool. Sprinkle with the thyme sprigs.

FETA, MINT & PINE NUT BOREKS

MAKES 16

- ½ cup pine nuts
- ⅓ cup olive oil, plus extra for greasing
- 1 onion, finely chopped
- 2 tablespoons chopped mint
- 2 tablespoons chopped parsley
- 1 garlic clove, crushed
- 7 oz feta cheese
- 4 sheets phyllo pastry
- Salt and freshly ground black pepper

1. Lightly toast the pine nuts in a dry skillet, shaking the skillet to evenly color. Transfer to a board and coarsely chop. Heat 2 tablespoons of the oil in the skillet and gently sauté the onion for 5 minutes to soften. Add the mint, parsley, and garlic and sauté for another 1 minute. Transfer to a bowl and stir in the pine nuts. Crumble in the feta and season lightly. Let cool.

2. Preheat the oven to 425°F and lightly grease a cookie sheet.

3. Lightly brush one pastry sheet with a little oil. Place a second sheet on top and brush lightly with a little more oil. Cut the pastry in half lengthwise, then into quarters in the opposite direction to make eight squares.

4. Place a teaspoonful of the filling along one long edge of a square, leaving a ½-inch space at the ends. Fold the ends inward and roll up the filling in the pastry to make a log shape. Transfer to the prepared cookie sheet and shape the remaining seven squares in the same way, using half the filling. Use the remaining pastry and filling to make more boreks.

5. Brush lightly with oil and bake in the preheated oven for about 20 minutes, until deep golden. Serve warm.

RAISIN & FENNEL COOKIES

- -

Savory cookies with just a touch of sweetness from the raisins, these are perfectly paired with cream cheese.

MAKES 16

- 1 shallot, finely chopped
- 1 cup spelt flour, plus extra for dusting
- ¾ cup rolled oats
- 1½ teaspoons fennel seed, lightly crushed
- ½ teaspoon sea salt
- 4 tablespoons salted butter, cut into pieces, plus extra for greasing
- 3 tablespoons finely chopped raisins
- ¼–⅓ cup cold water

1. Preheat the oven to 350°F and lightly grease two large cookie sheets.

2. Put the shallot, flour, oats, seed, and salt in a bowl and add the butter. Rub in with the fingertips until the mixture resembles fine bread crumbs. Add the raisins and the measured cold water and mix to a firm dough, adding a dash more water if the dough feels dry.

3. Thinly roll out the dough on a lightly floured surface until about 1 inch thick. Cut out circles using a 3-inch cutter. Place on the prepared cookie sheets, spacing them slightly apart, and reroll the scraps to make more.

4. Bake in the preheated oven for 15–20 minutes or until just beginning to color around the edges. Transfer to a wire rack to cool. Serve with soft cheeses.

CHORIZO & CHIVE PUFFS

MAKES 16

- 4 oz chorizo sausage
- 2 tablespoons tomato paste
- ½ cup milk, plus extra to glaze
- ⅓ cup chopped chives
- 2 cups all-purpose flour, plus extra for dusting
- 1 tablespoon baking powder
- 3 tablespoons salted butter, cut into small pieces, plus extra for greasing

1. Preheat the oven to 425°F and lightly grease a cookie sheet.

2. Chop the chorizo sausage as finely as possible. (Alternatively use a food processor to finely chop.) Beat the tomato paste with all but 2 tablespoons of the milk and the chives.

3. Put the flour and baking powder in a bowl and add the butter. Rub in with the fingertips until the mixture resembles fine bread crumbs. Add the chorizo and milk mixture and mix to a soft dough, adding the remaining milk if the dough feels dry. (Alternatively, use a food processor to blend the butter and flour, then blend in the milk mixture.)

4. Turn out onto a lightly floured surface and roll out to a square shape about ¾ inch thick. Trim off the edges. Using a sharp, floured knife or pizza wheel, cut the dough into 1¾-inch-wide lengths. Cut the dough across in the opposite direction to make small squares.

5. Transfer to the prepared cookie sheet, spacing them slightly apart. Brush with milk and bake in the preheated oven for 15 minutes, until risen and golden. Serve warm or cold, split and buttered.

PESTO & PECORINO BITES

MAKES 32

- 1¾ cups all-purpose flour, plus extra for dusting
- ¾ cup plus 2 tablespoons (1¾ sticks) salted butter, cut into small pieces, plus extra for greasing
- 2¼ cups coarsely grated Pecorino or Parmesan cheese
- 1 egg, separated, plus 1 egg yolk
- ¼ cup sun-dried tomato pesto
- Freshly ground black pepper
- ⅓ cup drained and chopped sun-dried tomatoes in oil
- 10 pitted ripe black olives, chopped
- Small basil leaves, to garnish

1. Put the flour in a bowl and add the butter. Rub in with the fingertips until the mixture resembles coarse bread crumbs. Stir in the cheese and both egg yolks and mix to a dough. (Alternatively use a food processor to blend the flour and butter, then add the cheese and egg yolk to make a dough.) Wrap and chill for at least 30 minutes.

2. Preheat the oven to 350°F and lightly grease a large cookie sheet.

3. Roll out the dough on a lightly floured surface to a 10 x 19-inch rectangle. Cut in half. Spread one half with the tomato pesto and season with plenty of black pepper. Neaten the edges and cut widthwise into eight thin strips. Make four cuts into the opposite direction to make 32 small rectangles. Transfer to the prepared cookie sheet, spacing the pieces slightly apart.

4. Brush with beaten egg white and arrange a few pieces of sun-dried tomato and olive down the centers. Season with black pepper and bake in the preheated oven for 15–20 minutes, until just turning pale golden. Let cool slightly and serve warm, garnished with basil leaves.

OLIVE & PARMESAN GRISSINI

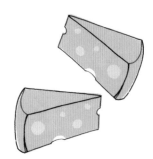

MAKES 30
- 3⅔ cups white bread flour, plus extra for dusting
- 2 teaspoons active dry yeast
- 1 teaspoon sea salt, plus extra for sprinkling
- 1 cup finely grated fresh Parmesan cheese
- 3 tablespoons extra-virgin olive oil, plus extra for greasing
- 1¼ cups tepid water
- Semolina, for sprinkling
- 15 pitted ripe black olives, finely chopped
- Beaten egg, to glaze

1. Put the flour, yeast, salt, cheese, and olive oil in a bowl and add the measured water. Mix to form a dough, adding a dash more water if the dough is dry and crumbly. Knead on a lightly floured surface for 10 minutes, until smooth and elastic. Place in a lightly oiled bowl, cover with plastic wrap, and let rise in a warm place for about 50–60 minutes, until the dough has doubled in size.

2. Preheat the oven to 425°F. Lightly grease two cookie sheets and sprinkle with semolina. Turn out the dough onto a lightly floured surface and knead in the olives until evenly distributed. Cover with a cloth and let sit for 10 minutes.

3. Roll out the dough to a rectangle measuring about 8 x 12 inches. Cut across the dough into thin strips and transfer the strips to the prepared cookie sheets, stretching them slightly and spacing them about ½ inch apart.

4. Brush with beaten egg and sprinkle with extra semolina and a litte sea salt. Bake in the preheated oven for about 15 minutes, until golden. If necessary, remove the baked grissini from the edges of the sheets and return to the oven for another few minutes. Transfer to a wire rack to cool.

5. These are best served on the day they're baked and can be warmed through to re-crisp.

CHEESE & TOMATO BITES

- -

These cheese-filled wafers are perfect served as appetizers or why not add them to lunchboxes as a tasty savory snack?

MAKES 30
- 1⅓ cups all-purpose flour, plus extra for dusting
- ½ teaspoon baking powder
- 6 tablespoons butter, plus extra for greasing
- 1 teaspoon celery salt (optional)
- 2 tablespoons ketchup

Filling
- ½ cup cream cheese
- 1 tablespoon snipped chives
- Salt and freshly ground black pepper

1. Preheat the oven to 400°F and lightly grease two cookie sheets.

2. Place the flour and baking powder in a bowl. Blend in the butter until the mixture resembles fine bread crumbs. Stir in the celery salt. if using, then add the ketchup and mix to form a stiff dough.

3. Roll out on a lightly floured surface and cut into 1-inch wafers with a knife or cookie cutter. Arrange on the prepared cookie sheets and bake in the preheated oven for 10–12 minutes, until golden. Let sit on the cookie sheets for a few minutes to slightly harden, then transfer to a wire rack to completely cool.

4. Beat together the cream cheese and chives and season to taste. Use to sandwich together two wafers. Fill just prior to serving.

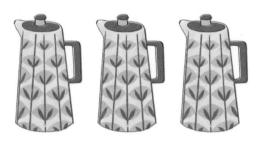

SESAME CHEESE TWISTS

MAKES 14
- 3½ oz cheddar cheese
- ½ cup (1 stick) butter, softened, plus extra for greasing
- 1⅔ cups all-purpose flour, plus extra for dusting
- Beaten egg, to glaze
- 2 tablespoons sesame seed

1. Preheat the oven to 400°F and lightly grease two cookie sheets.

2. Finely shred the cheese, using the fine shredder attachment of a food processor.

3. Remove the shredding disk and insert the metal mixing blade. Place the butter in the food processor with the cheese and process until pale and creamy. Add the flour and process until the mixture comes together to form a ball of dough.

4. Roll out the dough on a lightly floured surface to about ⅛ inch thick. Cut into strips about 6 inches long and 2 inches wide. Take two strips at a time and twist together, pinching the ends.

5. Arrange on the prepared cookie sheets. Brush with beaten egg and sprinkle with sesame seed. Bake in the preheated oven for 10–12 minutes, until pale golden, 10–12 minutes. Let sit on the cookie sheets for a few minutes to slightly harden, then transfer to a wire rack to completely cool.

BLUE CHEESE & POPPY SEED SLICES

- -

Tangy and tasty, try serving these savory cookies with a little butter, some grapes, and a cocktail or a glass of Port.

MAKES 25-30
- 1¼ cups all-purpose flour
- ½ cup (1 stick) butter, at room temperature
- 2½ oz mild soft blue cheese
- 2 tablespoons poppy seed

1. Put the flour, butter, and cheese into a bowl and mix well together. Place the mixture on plastic wrap and shape into a cylinder 1¾ inches in diameter. Chill until firm.

2. Preheat the oven to 350°F. Unwrap the dough and roll in the poppy seed. Cut into slices and place 1¼ inches apart on a nonstick cookie sheet.

3. Bake in the preheated oven for about 10 minutes, until lightly browned. Let sit on the cookie sheet for a few minutes to slightly harden, then transfer to a wire rack to completely cool.

PIZZA CHUNKS

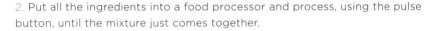

MAKES 24-30

- 1⅓ cups all-purpose flour
- ½ cup plus 2 tablespoons (1¼ sticks) butter
- ¼ cup grated Parmesan cheese
- ¼ cup shredded sharp cheddar cheese
- 1 tablespoon tomato paste
- ½ cup sun-dried tomatoes, coarsely chopped
- 1–2 teaspoons Italian dried mixed herbs
- 1 egg yolk
- 1 tablespoon water

1. Preheat the oven to 350°F.

2. Put all the ingredients into a food processor and process, using the pulse button, until the mixture just comes together.

3. Roll out the dough between sheets of parchment paper to a large rectangle shape.

4. Remove the top piece of parchment paper and lift the dough, using the bottom paper, onto a cookie sheet. Keep the bottom piece of paper in place. Using a fork or pastry wheel, mark lightly into squares or bars.

5. Bake in the preheated oven for about 10–15 minutes, until lightly browned. Transfer on the parchment paper to a wire rack and let cool, then break into pieces along the perforations.

SPICED PALMIERS

MAKES ABOUT 35

- 2 tablespoons olive oil, plus extra for greasing
- 1 small onion, finely chopped
- 2 teaspoons cumin seed, lightly crushed
- 1 teaspoon fennel seed, lightly crushed
- ½ teaspoon dried red pepper flakes
- ½ teaspoon sea salt, plus extra to sprinkle
- ¼ cup finely chopped cilantro
- 1 lb puff pastry
- Flour, for dusting
- Beaten egg, to glaze

1. Heat the oil in a skillet and gently sauté the onion for 5 minutes, until softened. Add the spices and salt and sauté for another 2 minutes. Transfer to a bowl, stir in the cilantro, and let cool.

2. Roll out the pastry on a lightly floured surface to a 10 x 14-inch rectangle. Brush with beaten egg and spread with the spice mixture in an even layer. Roll up the pastry, starting from a long side to shape a neat log. Wrap in plastic wrap and freeze for 1 hour.

3. Preheat the oven to 425°F and lightly grease two cookie sheets.

4. Trim off the ends of the pastry log to neaten. Using a sharp knife, cut the log across into ½-inch-wide slices. Roll the slices lightly with a rolling pin to flatten and space slightly apart on the prepared cookie sheets. Brush with beaten egg and sprinkle with extra sea salt.

5. Bake in the preheated oven for 12–15 minutes, until risen and golden. If the palmiers start to puff up in the centers during cooking, flatten them down with a spatula. Serve warm or transfer to a wire rack and let cool.

6. These are best served on the day they're baked.

VANILLA ROSEWATER SABLES P153

WITH A TWIST

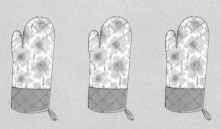

CITRUS CREAM CLOUDS

MAKES 18

- ¾ cup (1½ sticks) butter
- 1 teaspoon finely grated lime zest
- ⅔ cup confectioners' sugar
- 1 cups all-purpose flour
- ⅓ cup cornstarch

Filling

- ½ cup (1 stick) unsalted butter, at room temperature

- 1 teaspoon vanilla extract
- 1 teaspoon finely grated orange zest
- 1 teaspoon finely grated lemon zest
- 1¼ cups confectioners' sugar, sifted, plus extra for dusting

1. Beat together the butter, lime zest, and confectioners' sugar until smooth and creamy. Stir in the flour and cornstarch and knead until smooth. Wrap in plastic wrap and chill for 30 minutes, until firm.

2. Preheat the oven to 350°F and line three cookie sheets with parchment paper.

3. Roll out half the dough between sheets of parchment paper. Using a flower-shape cutter or a cutter of your choice cut out eighteen 1¾-inch shapes. Add any scraps of dough to the remaining dough and roll out as before and cut out eighteen 2½-inch shapes.

4. Place the shapes 1 inch apart on cookie sheets lined with parchment paper. Bake in the preheated oven for about 5–6 minutes for small shapes and 7–8 minutes for large shapes, until lightly browned. Let sit on the cookie sheets for a few minutes to slightly harden, then transfer to a wire rack to completely cool.

5. Put all the filling ingredients into a bowl and beat together until smooth and creamy.

6. Either pipe or spread the filling on each of the larger cookies. Top each one with a smaller cookie. Dust with confectioners' sugar to serve.

LADY GREY TEA COOKIES

Lady Grey tea is similar to Earl Grey but with the addition of orange and lemon peel. Serve these sugary slices with a nice cup of tea.

MAKES 18-20
- 6 tablespoons unsalted butter, at room temperature
- ¼ cup firmly packed light brown sugar
- 1 tablespoon Lady Grey tea leaves
- 1 egg white
- 1¼ cups all-purpose flour, plus extra for dusting
- Demerara sugar or other raw sugar, for sprinkling

1. Put the butter and sugar into a bowl and beat together until creamy. Stir in the tea leaves. Beat in the egg white. Fold in the flour to make a soft but not sticky dough.

2. Roll the dough into a cylinder on a lightly floured work surface. Flatten slightly to make a cross section that looks like a ladyfinger cookie with rounded ends. Wrap carefully in plastic wrap and chill for about 30 minutes or until firm enough to slice.

3. Preheat the oven to 375°F. Line three cookie sheets with some parchment paper.

4. Cut into thin slices and place on the prepared cookie sheets. Sprinkle each cookie with demerara sugar. Bake in the preheated oven for 10–15 minutes, until lightly browned.

CHERRY STREUSEL SLICE

MAKES ABOUT 15

- I (15-oz) can pitted red or black cherries in light syrup
- 4 teaspoons cornstarch
- ¾ cup plus 2 tablespoons superfine sugar
- 2 cups all-purpose flour
- 2 teaspoons baking powder
- I teaspoon ground allspice
- ¾ cup (1½ sticks) salted butter, cut into small pieces
- ⅓ cup ground almonds
- I egg yolk
- Confectioners' sugar, for dusting

1. Preheat the oven to 350°F.

2. Drain the cherries, reserving two-thirds of the juice. Coarsely chop the cherries. Blend 2 tablespoons of the juice in a saucepan with the cornstarch. Add the remaining reserved juice and 2 tablespoons of the superfine sugar and heat gently, stirring, until the mixture is thick and bubbling. Stir in the cherries and heat for another 1 minute. Remove from the heat and let cool.

3. Put the flour, baking powder, and allspice in a food processor. Add the butter and blend until the mixture resembles coarse bread crumbs. Add the remaining superfine sugar and ground almonds and blend briefly again. Measure out 1¼ cups of the mixture and add the egg yolk to the remainder in the processor. Blend to a dough.

4. Spread the dough into a shallow 7 x 12½-inch baking pan, pressing it down firmly in a thin, even layer with your fingers. Spoon the cherry mixture on top and sprinkle with the crumbs.

5. Bake in the preheated oven for 40 minutes or until the crumble is golden. Let cool in the pan. Sprinkle with confectioners' sugar and serve cut into squares.

COFFEE CREAM CRISPS

MAKES 15
- 2 teaspoons instant espresso coffee powder
- 1¼ cups all-purpose flour, plus extra for dusting
- ½ cup (1 stick) salted butter, cut into pieces, plus extra for greasing
- ½ cup confectioners' sugar, plus extra for dusting
- 1 egg yolk
- ⅔ cup heavy cream
- 2 tablespoons coffee-flavored liqueur (optional)
- Cocoa mix or cocoa powder, for dusting

1. Put the coffee and flour in a food processor and add the butter. Blend until the mixture resembles bread crumbs. Add ⅓ cup of the sugar and the egg yolk and blend to a dough. Wrap and chill for at least 1 hour.

2. Preheat the oven to 350°F and lightly grease two cookie sheets.

3. Roll out the dough thinly on a lightly floured surface (it should be no more than about ⅛ inch thick) and cut out circles, using a 2-inch cutter. Reroll the scraps to make more.

4. Space slightly apart on the prepared cookie sheets. Bake in the preheated oven for 10 minutes, until turning pale golden. Let sit on the cookie sheets for a few minutes to slightly harden, then transfer to a wire rack to completely cool.

5. Whip the cream with the remaining confectioners' sugar and the liqueur, if using, until just forming peaks. Use to sandwich together the cookies.

6. Dust with extra confectioners' sugar, then a little cocoa mix or cocoa powder. Let sit for 2–3 hours, until firm, before serving.

LAVENDER SCENTED SHORTBREAD

MAKES 18-20

- 4 dried lavender flowers, natural and unsprayed
- 1 cup (2 sticks) butter
- 1¾ cups all-purpose flour
- ¾ cup rice flour
- Pinch of salt
- Extra lavender flowers and superfine sugar, for decoration

1. Line two cookie sheets with wax paper.

2. Put the sugar and lavender in a food processor and blend for about 10 seconds.

3. Cream together the butter and sugar until light and fluffy, then stir in the flours, and salt until the mixture resembles bread crumbs.

4. Using your hands, gather the dough together and knead until it forms a ball. Roll into a log shape and then shape into a long rectangle about 2 inches thick. Wrap in plastic wrap and chill for about 30 minutes or until firm.

5. Preheat the oven to 375°F. Slice the dough into ½ inch squares and place on the prepared cookie sheets. Bake in the preheated oven for 15-20 minutes or until pale golden. Sprinkle with extra sugar and let sit on the cookie sheets for a few minutes, then transfer to a wire rack to cool completely. Decorate with extra lavender flowers before serving.

FRENCH MACAROONS

- - - - - - - - - - - - - - -

MAKES 24

- Butter, for greasing
- ⅓ cup confectioners' sugar
- ⅔ cup ground almonds
- 2 egg whites
- ½ cup superfine sugar
- Pink and green food coloring

1. Grease and line two cookie sheets with parchment paper.

2. Put the confectioners' sugar in a food processor with the ground almonds and blend to a fine consistency.

3. Put the egg whites in a thoroughly clean bowl and whisk until holding stiff peaks. Gradually whisk in the superfine sugar, a tablespoonful at a time, and whisking well after each addition, until thick and glossy.

4. Divide the mixture equally between two bowls and add a few drops of food coloring to each bowl. Divide the almond mixture equally between the two bowls and use a metal spoon to stir the mixtures gently to combine.

5. Place one colour in a pastry bag fitted with a ½-inch plain tip and pipe twelve 1¼-inch circles onto one prepared cookie sheet. Tap the cookie sheet firmly to smooth the surfaces of the macaroons. Wash and dry the bag and piping tip and pipe twelve circles in the second color onto the other cookie sheet. Let sit for 30 minutes.

6. Meanwhile, preheat the oven 325°F.

7. Bake the macaroons in the preheated oven for about 15 minutes, or until the surfaces feel crisp. Let cool before carefully peeling away the paper.

MACADAMIA, FIG & GINGER CANTUCCINI

MAKES 22

- 2 eggs
- ⅔ cup superfine sugar
- 2 cups all-purpose flour, plus extra for dusting
- 1 teaspoon baking powder
- Grated zest of 1 lemon
- ⅔ cup macadamia nuts, toasted and chopped
- ½ cup finely chopped dried figs
- ⅓ cup finely chopped crystallized (candied) ginger
- Butter, for greasing

1. Put the eggs and sugar in a bowl and, using an electric hand mixer, beat together for 5 minutes, until pale and thick. Sift in the flour and baking powder and stir into the egg mixture with the remaining ingredients, except the butter, to form a soft, slightly sticky dough.

2. Preheat the oven to 300°F and lightly grease a cookie sheet.

3. Transfer half of the dough to a well-floured surface and roll into a 3 x 12-inch flattened log. Transfer to the prepared cookie sheet. Bake in the preheated oven for 30 minutes.

4. Remove from the oven and reduce the temperature to 300°F. Use a serrated knife to cut the dough diagonally into slices ½ inch thick and lay them flat on the cookie sheet. Bake for another 20–25 minutes, until golden. Let sit on the cookie sheets for a few minutes to slightly harden, then transfer to a wire rack to completely cool. Repeat with the remaining dough to make 22 cookies.

LEMONY CORNMEAL COOKIES

MAKES 18
- ½ cup superfine sugar
- I cup ground almonds
- ¾ cup cornmeal
- ¼ cup cornstarch
- ¾ cup (I½ sticks) salted butter, softened, plus extra for greasing
- 2 eggs
- Finely grated zest of I lemon, plus 2 teaspoons juice
- I cup confectioners' sugar
- sugar sprinkles, to decorate

1. Preheat the oven to 350°F. Grease 18 sections of two tart pans. If you have only one pan, save one-third of the dough to bake separately.

2. Put the superfine sugar, ground almonds, cornmeal, cornstarch, ½ cup (1 stick) of the butter, the eggs, and the lemon zest in a bowl and beat well until smooth.

3. Spoon into the prepared pan sections and bake in the preheated oven for 15–20 minutes, until slightly risen. Let cool in the pans, then twist out of the pans.

4. Beat the remaining butter with the confectioners' sugar and lemon juice until smooth and creamy. Place in a pastry bag fitted with a small star tip and pipe swirls into the centers of the cookies. Decorate with sugar sprinkles.

MULLED WINE
COOKIES

These festive fancies are great on winter nights round the fire, or by a Christmas tree. With warming cinnamon, they are sure to bring cheer.

MAKES ABOUT 25

- I cup raisins
- ½ cup dried cranberries
- ⅔ cup red wine
- ⅓ cup red currant or grape jelly
- I teaspoon ground cinnamon
- ¼ teaspoon ground cloves
- good pinch of chili powder
- ½ cup walnuts
- ½ cup whole blanched almonds
- 4 oz rum-flavored or semisweet chocolate
- ⅔ cup all-purpose flour
- ½ teaspoon baking powder
- Finely grated zest of I orange
- 4 tablespoons unsalted butter, melted, plus extra for greasing
- I egg
- Confectioners' sugar, for dusting

1. Put the raisins and cranberries in a small, heavy saucepan with the wine, jelly, and spices. Heat until the jelly dissolves, then bring to a boil and boil for 2–3 minutes, until the syrup is reduced by about half. Let cool.

2. Preheat the oven to 350°F and lightly grease a large cookie sheet.

3. Chop the nuts and chocolate. Mix in a bowl with the flour, baking powder, orange zest, melted butter, egg, and fruit mixture to make a dough. Place teaspoonfuls of the dough, spaced slightly apart, on the prepared cookie sheet.

4. Bake in the preheated oven for about 20 minutes, until the cookies have spread slightly. Let sit on the cookie sheets for a few minutes to slightly harden, then transfer to a wire rack to completely cool.

5. Dust generously with confectioners' sugar.

STENCILED COOKIES

MAKES 10
- Butter, for greasing
- I quantity Spicy Gingerbread dough, chilled (see page 41)
- Flour, for dusting
- I quantity Quick Buttercream (see page 10)
- Confectioners' sugar, for dusting

1. Preheat the oven to 350°F and lightly grease two cookie sheets.

2. Thinly roll out the cookie dough on a lightly floured surface and, using a 2½-inch round cookie cutter, cut out circles. Place on the prepared cookie sheets, spacing them slightly apart, and reroll the scraps to make extras.

3. Bake in the preheated oven for 12 minutes or until the dough has risen slightly and is beginning to darken around the edges. Let sit on the cookie sheets for a few minutes to slightly harden, then transfer to a wire rack to completely cool.

4. Sandwich the cookies together with the buttercream.

5. Make a template by cutting out a design, using a craft knife, on a 3-inch circle of paper. Curvy lines, dots, numbers, and figures all look effective.

6. Lay the template over a cookie and dust with plenty of confectioners' sugar. Carefully lift the template away, shake off the excess sugar, and repeat the decoration on the other cookies.

FROSTED FRUIT
COOKIES

- -

MAKES 20
- Butter, for greasing
- 1 quantity Vanilla Cookie dough, chilled (see page 40)
- Flour, for dusting
- 1 egg white
- 2 cups mixture of red currants, black currants, and white currants, plus extra sprigs for decoration (or if not available, use blueberries)
- ⅔ cup blueberries
- ⅓ cup superfine sugar
- 1¼ cups heavy or whipping cream
- 2 teaspoons vanilla extract

1. Preheat the oven to 350°F and lightly grease a large cookie sheet.

2. Thinly roll out the cookie dough on a lightly floured surface and, using a 3½-inch fluted, round cookie cutter, cut out circles. Place on the prepared cookie sheet, spacing them slightly apart, and reroll the scraps to make extras.

3. Bake in the preheated oven for 15 minutes or until pale golden. Let sit on the cookie sheets for a few minutes to slightly harden, then transfer to a wire rack to completely cool.

4. Line a baking pan or cookie sheet with parchment paper. Lightly beat the egg white in a shallow dish to break it up. Brush all the fruits, including the sprigs, with the egg white and then sprinkle with the sugar. Place on the prepared pan or cookie sheet and let dry for at least 30 minutes.

5. Whip the cream with the vanilla extract and pipe or spoon onto the cookies.

6. Pile the sugar-frosted fruits onto the cream and place a cluster of currants on top of each for decoration.

VANILLA ROSEWATER SABLES

MAKES ABOUT 20

- 2¼ cups all-purpose flour, sifted, plus extra for dusting
- ¾ cup plus 2 tablespoons (1¾ sticks) chilled unsalted butter, diced, plus extra for greasing
- ¾ cup confectioners' sugar, sifted
- 2 egg yolks
- 2 teaspoons vanilla extract

Pink buttercream
- 4 tablespoons unsalted butter, softened
- ⅔ cup confectioners' sugar, sifted, plus extra for dusting
- 1 teaspoon boiling water
- Few drops of pink food coloring
- 1–2 teaspoons rosewater

1. Put the flour and butter in a food processor and blend until the mixture resembles bread crumbs. Add the sugar, egg yolks, and vanilla extract and blend to make a smooth dough. Wrap in plastic wrap and chill for an hour.

2. Preheat the oven to 400°F and lightly grease two cookie sheets.

3. Roll out half the dough on a lightly floured surface to about ⅛ inch thick, and cut out heart shapes using a 1¾-inch heart-shape cutter. Space slightly apart on one prepared cookie sheet. Roll out the remaining dough and shape more hearts. Put on the second cookie sheet and reroll the scraps for extra.

4. Bake in the preheated oven for about 8 minutes, or until just beginning to turn golden around the edges. Let sit on the cookie sheets for a few minutes to slightly harden, then transfer to a wire rack to completely cool.

5. Make the buttercream by beating together the butter and confectioners' sugar in a bowl until smooth. Add the measured water, the pink food coloring, and enough of the rosewater to create a delicate flavor, then beat until pale and creamy. Use the buttercream to sandwich together the cookies. Serve lightly dusted with confectioners' sugar.

ICECREAM SANDWICH

- - - - - - - - - - - - - - - - - -

MAKES 10

- ½ cup (1 stick) unsalted butter at room temperature
- ½ cup plus 1 tablespoon superfine sugar
- 1 egg, beaten
- 1 ⅔ cups all-purpose flour
- ¼ cup unsweetened cocoa powder, sifted
- ⅔ cup semisweet chocolate chips
- Chocolate or vanilla ice cream

1. Preheat the oven to 350°F. Line a cookie sheet with parchment paper.

2. Cream together the butter and sugar and beat in the egg. Stir in the flour, cocoa, and chocolate chips to make a firm dough. Roll out on parchment paper. Cut into 20 rectangles each 3½ x 2 inches.

3. Place on the prepared cookie sheet. Bake in the preheated oven for about 15 minutes. Let sit on the cookie sheets for a few minutes to slightly harden, then transfer to a wire rack to completely cool.

4. To make the ice cream cookies, spread two good spoonfuls of softened ice cream on a cookie and press a second cookie on top. Squeeze so the filling reaches the edges.

5. Eat immediately or wrap individually in aluminium foil and freeze. Store for up to two weeks in the freezer.

INDEX

almonds
almond & white chocolate
kisses 61
almond butter cookies 54
biscotti 35
cherry & almond cookies
29
cherry streusel slice 142-3
chocolate kisses 85
chocolate refrigerator bars
88-9
fig & date rolls 68
Florentines 58-9
French macaroons 146
fruit & nut cookies 49
gluten free almond
macaroons 61
japonais 22
lemony cornmeal cookies
148-9
mulled wine cookies 150
ricciarelle cookies 46-7
thumbprint cookies 12, 30
apples
tangy apple squares 20-1

baby shower cookies 108-9
bacon, thyme & herb sticks
124-5
bananas
banana walnut cookies 62
bees & hives 113
beetroot
red velvet cookies 78-9

biscotti 35
triple chocolate biscotti 98
blackcurrants
frosted fruit cookies 152
blueberries
frosted fruit cookies 152
buttercream 10
cars 111
gingerbread men 116
little dinos 107
pink champagne cocktails
102-3
stenciled cookies 151
vanilla rosewater sables
138, 153
buttermilk
spicy buttermilk cookies
42

caramel pine nut slices 87
caramelitas 67
caraway seeds
golden raisin & caraway
cookies 57
cardamom & orange
madeleines 38-9
cheese
bacon, thyme & herb sticks
124-5
blue cheese & poppy seed
slices 134
cheese & tomato bites 132
feta, mint & pine nut
boreks 126

olive & Parmesan grissini
130-1
pesto & pecorino bites 129
pizza chunks 135
red velvet cookies 78-9
sesame cheese twists 133
whoopies 94-5
cherries
cherry & almond cookies
29
cherry streusel slice 142-3
Florentines 58-9
fruit & nut cookies 49
chillies
chocolate & chile cookies
81
chocolate
almond & white chocolate
kisses 61
bees & hives 113
caramel pine nut slices 87
caramelitas 67
chocolate brownie cookies
72-3
chocolate butter cookies
84
chocolate & chile cookies
81
chocolate chip cookies
with ginger 90
chocolate cigars 96
chocolate cinnamon
crunchies 76
chocolate cookies 40

chocolate Florentines 99
chocolate and ginger
   cookies 81
chocolate ginger yo yos 18
chocolate jumble crunchies
   82-3
chocolate kisses 85
chocolate macaroons 91
chocolate Maryland
   cookies 74
chocolate refrigerator bars
   88-9
chocolate ring cookies 97
chocolate spice cookies 92
chocolate, vanilla and
   hazelnut cookies 80
Christmas tree decorations
   120-1
chunky chocolate cookies
   75
Florentines 58-9
glazed chocolate ginger
   hearts 93
icecream sandwich 154-5
mint chocolate sandwiches
   86
mulled wine cookies 150
peanut butter and
   chocolate chip cookies 56
red velvet cookies 78-9
spots & stripes 117
thumbprint cookies 12, 30
triple chocolate biscotti 98
triple chocolate cookies
   80
white chocolate &
   lemongrass cookies 77
white chocolate rocky road
   88
whoopies 94-5

chorizo and chive puffs 128
Christmas baubles 105
Christmas tree decorations
   120-1
chunky oat cookies 37
cinnamon
   chocolate cinnamon
      crunchies 76
   Christmas tree decorations
      120-1
   Cinnamon ginger cookies
      18
   mulled wine cookies 150
   tangy apple squares 20-1
citrus cream clouds 140
classic shortbread 19
coconut
   coconut gems 64-5
   white chocolate rocky road
      88
coffee
   coffee cream crisps 144
   japonais 22
coffee beans, chocolate 91
cornmeal
   lemony cornmeal cookies
      148-9
cranberries
   chocolate refrigerator bars
      88-9
   Florentines 58-9
   mulled wine cookies 150
custard creams 32-3

dates
   fig & date rolls 68
dried fruit
   chocolate refrigerator bars
      88-9
   chocolate spice cookies 92

Florentines 58-9
fruit & nut cookies 49

egg whites
   beating 8

fall cookies 118
fennel seeds
   fennel & orange cookies 57
   raisin & fennel cookies 127
   spiced palmiers 136-7
figs
   chocolate refrigerator bars
      88-9
   fig & date rolls 68
   macadamia, fig & ginger
      cantuccini 147
Florentines 58-9
   chocolate Florentines 99
fondant
   3 D winter wonderland 104
   baby shower cookies
      108-9
   bees & hives 113
   cars 111
   ghosts 119
   little dinos 107
   spots & stripes 117
   wise old owls 110
French honey & fruit cookies
   50

ghosts 119
ginger
   chocolate chip cookies
      with ginger 90
   chocolate and ginger
      cookies 81
   chocolate ginger yo yos 18
   cinnamon ginger cookies 18

gingerbread men 116
gingerbread night lights
  114–15
glazed chocolate ginger
  hearts 93
macadamia, fig & ginger
  cantuccini 147
preserved ginger pumpkin
  cookies 26–7
shooting stars 106
spicy gingerbread 41, 104
spots & stripes 117
stenciled cookies 151
sticky ginger cookies 28
whoopies with mascarpone
  & ginger filling 95
glitter icing
lacy butterflies 112
gluten free almond
macaroons 61
golden raisins
golden raisin & caraway
  cookies 57
white chocolate &
  lemongrass cookies 77
graham crackers
chocolate jumble crunchies
  82–3
chocolate refrigerator bars
  88–9

hazelnuts
chocolate refrigerator bars
  88–9
chocolate ring cookies 97
chocolate, vanilla and
  hazelnut cookies 80
honey
French honey & fruit
  cookies 50

sunflower seed cookies
  14–15

icecream sandwich 154–5

japonais 22
jelly beans
baby shower cookies
  108–9
jelly filled cookies 24

lacy butterflies 112
Lady Grey tea cookies 141
langues de chat 17
lavender scented shortbread
  145
lemongrass
white chocolate &
  lemongrass cookies 77
lemons
citrus cream clouds 140
fig & date rolls 68
golden raisin & caraway
  cookies 57
lemon cookies 23
lemon macadamia nut
  cookies 63
lemony cornmeal cookies
  148–9
melting moments 16
ricciarelle cookies 46–7

macadamia nuts
lemon macadamia nut
  cookies 63
macadamia, fig & ginger
  cantuccini 147
macaroons
chocolate macaroons 91
French macaroons 146

madeleines
cardamom & orange
  madeleines 38–9
malted drop cookies 43
maple syrup oat bars 31
melting moments 16
meringue
pecan meringue crisps
  52–3
mint
feta, mint & pine nut
  boreks 126
mother's oat bars 25
mulled wine cookies 150

oats
caramelitas 67
chocolate ring cookies 97
chunky chocolate cookies
  75
chunky oat cookies 37
fruit & nut cookies 49
malted drop cookies 43
maple syrup oat bars 31
mother's oat bars 25
preserved ginger pumpkin
  cookies 26–7
sunflower seed cookies
  14–15
olives
olive & Parmesan grissini
  130–1
pesto & pecorino bites 129
oranges
biscotti 35
cardamom & orange
  madeleines 38–9
chocolate ginger yo yos 18
citrus cream clouds 140
fennel & orange cookies 57

melting moments 16
mulled wine cookies 150
orange and allspice hearts
121
whoopies 94-5

pâté sucrée
walnut barquettes 51
peanut butter
peanut butter and
chocolate chip cookies
56
peanut butter cookies 56
vanilla & peanut whoopies
60
pecans
caramelitas 67
pecan meringue crisps
52-3
pecan snaps 55
pesto & pecorino bites 129
phyllo pastry
feta, mint & pine nut
boreks 126
pine nuts
caramel pine nut slices 87
feta, mint & pine nut
boreks 126
Florentines 58-9
pink champagne cocktails
102-3
pistachio nuts
chocolate Florentines 99
pistachio cookies 48
white chocolate rocky road
88
pizza chunks 135
poppy seeds
blue cheese & poppy seed
slices 134

potatoes
bacon, thyme & herb sticks
124-5
preserved ginger pumpkin
cookies 26-7
puff pastry
spiced palmiers 136-7
tangy apple squares 20-1
pumpkin
preserved ginger pumpkin
cookies 26-7

raisins
chocolate Florentines 99
chunky chocolate cookies
75
golden raisin & caraway
cookies 57
mulled wine cookies 150
raisin and fennel cookies
127
white chocolate &
lemongrass cookies 77
raspberry jelly
jelly filled cookies 24
red velvet cookies 78-9
redcurrants
frosted fruit cookies 152
ricciarelle cookies 46-7
rosewater
vanilla rosewater sables
138, 153
royal icing 10
3 D winter wonderland 104
baby shower cookies 108-9
Christmas baubles 105
fall cookies 118
gingerbread night lights
114-15
lacy butterflies 112

sesame cheese twists 133
shooting stars 106
shortbread
classic shortbread 19
lavender scented
shortbread 145
spiced palmiers 136-7
spicy buttermilk cookies 42
spicy gingerbread 41
spots & stripes 117
stenciled cookies 151
sticky ginger cookies 28
sugar sprinkles
Christmas baubles 105
pink champagne cocktails
102-3
sunflower seed cookies 14-15

tangy apple squares 20-1
tea
Lady Grey tea cookies 141

vanilla & peanut whoopies
60
vanilla cookies 40
vanilla rosewater sables 153
walnut barquettes 51
wise old owls 110

wafer snaps 34
walnuts
banana walnut cookies 62
chocolate jumble crunchies
82-3
mulled wine cookies 150
walnut barquettes 51
walnut kisses 69
white chocolate
almond & white chocolate
kisses 61

bees & hives 113

chocolate jumble crunchies
    82-3

chocolate ring cookies 97

Florentines 58-9

glazed chocolate ginger
    hearts 93

red velvet cookies 78-9

triple chocolate biscotti 98

triple chocolate cookies 80

white chocolate &
lemongrass cookies 77

white chocolate rocky
    road 88

white currants
    frosted fruit cookies 152

whoopies 94-5
    mascarpone & ginger filling
    for 95
    vanilla & peanut whoopies
    60

GLOSSARY

- All-purpose flour = plain flour
- Allspice = mixed spice
- Apple pie mix = mixed spice
- Baking soda = bicarbonate of soda
- Cilantro = coriander
- Confectioners' sugar = icing sugar
- Cornmeal = polenta
- Cornstarch = cornflour
- Corn syrup = golden syrup
- Dark chocolate = plain chocolate
- Decorating tip = nozzle
- Fondant = fondant icing
- Frosting = icing
- Golden raisins = sultanas
- Jellyroll pan = Swiss roll tin
- Light brown sugar = muscovado sugar
- Light cream = single cream
- Pastry bag = piping bag
- Plastic wrap = clingfilm
- Preserved ginger = stem ginger
- Raw sugar = cane sugar
- Rolled oats = porridge oats
- Semisweet chocolate = plain chocolate
- Superfine sugar = caster sugar

PICTURE CREDITS

All photographs © Octopus Publishing Group. Ian Garlick 12; Ian Wallace 10, 44, 58, 89; Lis Parsons 2, 15, 21, 27, 33, 39, 47, 53, 65, 72, 79, 100, 103, 109, 114, 122,125, 131, 137, 143, 149, 155; Stephen Conroy 83; Will Heap 94, 138; William Shaw 7 left & right, 70, 120.